TO THE ONE

BY
MARNIE FREEMAN

For information, contact Ollin Media, Portland Oregon.
www.ToTheOneBook.com

Book Development Editor, Jan Black, The Black Brand.
www.TheBlackBrand.com

Book Editor, Randy Peyser, Author One Stop, Inc.
www.AuthorOneStop.com

Cover Design by Jan Black, The Black Brand.
www.TheBlackBrand.com.

Tree of Life Cover Illustration adapted from art of Liudmila Horvath.

Createspace Formatting by www.ebooklaunch.com

ISBN 978-0-578-14858-8

Ollin Media

Portland, Oregon

Dedicated to my grandmother,
Lucy Freeman McBride, my Grams,
who loved me with all of her heart, just as I am.

You will be with me forever.

TABLE OF CONTENTS

ACKNOWLEDGEMENTS

This book would not have been possible without the unending support of my true love, Rebecca Marie. We have spent twelve amazing years together including great challenges and exciting adventures. She is my best friend, my rock, and my 'go to.' I will be forever grateful that you chose to love me.

To Sophia and Gabby, I am so proud of both of you. You fill my days with joy and laughter. I never knew that I could love two little girls so much. You have been so very patient as I have worked to finish this book. Thank you.

I will be forever grateful to my parents for the love and home they provided for me. Their commitment to me is undeniable. My mother sat through hundreds of basketball games, softball games and track meets. No matter the time of night, she was there to talk. My dad taught me to work hard, laugh, and have a sense of humor. I love you both. You will always be in my heart.

If someone were to ask me, *who is your hero?,* I would unequivocally say my sister Jana. Even though Jana is my younger sister, she is a constant example of the type of person I hope to be - a model of love and service. I love you with all of my heart.

To all of my brothers and sisters, I love and thank you for your friendship and love. I have so many fun memories of love and laughter.

Without the support and vision of Jan Black, this book would have never been a reality. Thank you for seeing the value of my story and helping me to believe. You are a wizard with words, and an incredibly talented artist. Thank you for your countless hours of hard work writing, editing and bringing my story to life. The book cover is magnificent. I am so grateful to have you on my team.

A heartfelt thanks to Sara Goodman, Marnie Conti, and Deb Maccabee for your loving support and friendship, especially the last sixteen months as I have finished writing my book. All the late night talks, dinners, and your unending friendships have gotten me through the emotional highs and lows of life and finishing my book. Thank you.

A special thanks to an amazing editor, Randy Peyser. You took on this book and made suggestions and edits that took this book to a whole new level. Thank you for your brilliance.

Marnie Freeman

Introduction

Three Septembers, five events, and three wake-up calls convinced me to write this book, which originally was a journal I kept hidden and unread. The journal traced my path from my life as a happy Mormon kid to becoming an outcast lesbian woman. On these pages I said what I couldn't say out loud. Writing my story and feelings was the vent I used to release enough pressure to carry on without imploding.

The first event that led me to turn my journal into a book occurred on a September Sunday in 2011. A Unitarian speaker said, "When we look at the suicide rate of teenage and young adult gay and lesbian kids, we know that we can do better." Her words were like a kick to my gut. "We can do better" played in my head like a song on repeat. I couldn't shake it.

The second event happened the next day. I was driving to my medical clinic and listening to a CD by Jack Canfield, co-author of the *Chicken Soup for the Soul* ™ series, about finding your true purpose in life. I love my work as a Chinese Medicine practitioner. It is the path of my heart. However, for the six months before that day in September, I felt like something was missing. I realized as I listened to his CD that there was something else I was also meant to do.

The third event happened within an hour of the second. Before work that day, I stopped to keep an appointment I had made to have my back treated. I had been in pain for about ten weeks. The knot and heaviness from the "We can do better" message of the day before was still with me. Thoughts about my life purpose were also present, and the legacy I wanted to leave for my children. Something was out of balance, but I didn't know what it was.

I lay down on the table to be treated. When the practitioner's hands touched my back, a profound sadness came over me. A memory came out of nowhere of one of the most painful moments in my life - when I'd held a gun to my head because I did not feel that being gay was a life worth living.

The next forty minutes of treatment took me back in time to feel the pain as if it were happening all over again. There I was on the twelfth floor of a downtown Portland building in a group treatment room trying to control my tears so no one would notice. It was impossible. They flowed like a river.

As the tears ran down my face, a memory returned of something I had said at age seventeen. I was working a summer job in Carmel Valley, California, at Rana Creek Ranch. My boss had asked me what I wanted to do or be. It was the first time anyone had asked me that question, and I hadn't asked it of myself. The path was pretty clear. I would go to college, find a great Mormon man, be married in the Temple, and we would raise a bunch of happy kids who would do the same. Yes, there was the secret dread that I was gay, but at that time I was counting on God to take my attraction to women away and make me "normal."

I was surprised by my answer. "I want to be a counselor for gay and lesbian youth and young adults because their suicide rate is so high."

After blurting out my reply, which I believe happened because that is what I needed so desperately myself, I was terrified my boss would know my secret. I spent the next few minutes assuring him, and I think myself, that I was not gay.

I got up from the treatment table swallowing my sobs. I made it to my car before crumbling. How could I still have so much sadness and grief after so many years?

"We can do better." The phrase consumed me and transformed itself into "I can do better." I knew I had to finish my story -

this story, which I started so long ago in my journal, and that might just make a difference to even one person.

But I didn't finish writing my story. This was my first wake-up call.

A year rushed by. I lived a busy life and excused myself for not getting my book written.

The fourth event happened in September of 2012. I was alone at home and wanted to watch an action movie. Instead, I watched a documentary called *Wish Me Away*. It is country singer, Chely Wright's, coming out story. It was the first time I saw the level of suffering I had experienced in someone else. As I watched Chely deal with her family, her music community, her church, and her fears, heartache, loss of appetite and sleepless nights, I felt as if I were watching myself. Looking into her eyes as she was filming herself late at night made me feel as though I were looking into my own.

At the end of the movie, Chely said she came out because of the fourteen-year old kid in Iowa who was just like me. She had been that fourteen-year old kid. I had been that fourteen-year-old kid. If only there had been someone who could have reached out to me to let me know I was still okay, that God loved me all the same, and that I was still a worthy human being. At the time, I vaguely knew there were other gay and lesbian people in the world, but I truly believed I was the only gay Mormon kid.

The movie motivated me to finish my book. But I didn't get to it. This was my second wake-up call.

The fifth event occurred the following September. Jan Black was an acquaintance who had come to me for treatment. We were talking about finding one's greatness.

"Greatness to me is having dreams, working toward them with all of your heart, might and strength, and failing, then picking yourself up and doing it again," I said. "Greatness means never giving up on your dream, even if it takes a lifetime to accomplish it."

Jan asked, "What is your greatness?"

I knew my answer but I didn't want to tell her. I had never spoken it out loud and felt that by doing so, I would somehow morally obligate myself to go for it. I wasn't sure I was ready, but I took a breath and said, "Long ago I wrote a journal that I've imagined becoming a book."

"What's the book about?" she asked.

"I wrote a memoir about growing up in the Mormon Church as a gay kid," I said. "I know in the core of my being that I am meant to finish it but I haven't done it."

"I can help you make that happen," she said. At the time I didn't know she was a best-selling author and editor.

"I'll think about it and let you know my answer when you come back in two weeks," I said. I wasn't ready to commit, yet felt this was it, my third wake-up call.

Two weeks later, Jan returned, and I said, "Yes. I'm ready to do this." I told her this would be difficult because I would be opening many old wounds, not only for myself but also for my family. She smiled at me and said, "You can do this."

That day, before leaving my clinic, I emailed my journal to Jan. I was tempted to read it first but didn't. It had been years since I last looked at it. Only one other person had read it. What if Jan didn't think the journal was worth turning into a book?

Jan called me the next day, excited. She believed we could make it happen and, most importantly, she helped me believe it, too. Tears filled my eyes as I surrendered to my dream.

Getting this book into your hands has been both exhilarating and troubling. I have been afraid of the consequences of making my story public. A friend gave me Brene Brown's book, *Daring Greatly*. In it she speaks of her own fear and asks, "What is worth doing, even if you fail?"

I took her quote to heart, reciting it to myself many times each day on those dark days of fear. It is worth it to put my story out there, even if I fail. Why? Because I know there are many people out there just like me. The suicide rate for LGBT youth and young adults is four times higher than others and eight times higher for those from conservative religious communities. An LGBT life is taken by suicide every five hours, and for every one of those, twenty others attempt it.

My past has taught me that when I let myself feel my heartbreak, one painful day at a time, the light will return. I also discovered that facing the darkness changed me. It is what fueled my healing and enabled me to create the joyful life I live today with people I love and who love me.

I titled the book *To The One*, because it was the title of a pamphlet a Mormon Bishop had given to me in high school. It was written to the one who was gay, the one who was a disgrace and unworthy. It shamed me beyond where my own shame had already taken me.

I want to flip the meaning of *To The One*. This book is to the one who is gay, the one who is loved and worthy. It is written to help move you past any shame and into acceptance and unconditional love for yourself.

I can do better. We can do better. As frightening and revealing as it is to publish my story, my hope is to reach the one.

Chapter 1
I Have a Secret

When I was seventeen years old and kissing John Henderson on the couch in the family room of my parents' house, I told him a secret I had been hiding for years. It became the first of a string of tellings that slowly unraveled me like a hand-knit sweater whose stitches come undone.

John and I had just begun dating again after his return from a two-year mission to Argentina for the Mormon Church. It felt good to be together again, to pick up where we had left off. I was still a student at Salinas High School in California where John had been Student Body President a few years earlier. Like John, I was a Mormon from birth and our families followed the teachings religiously.

Before John left for Argentina, our time together had gone from group dating, because I wasn't yet sixteen, to one "official" date before he left.

John arrived in his best Sunday suit and tie, and I wore a long blue dress. We could have gone straight to church and fit right in. As we headed to his car, my parents waved us goodbye.

In honor of my love of author John Steinbeck, John took me to the Steinbeck House for dinner, a very popular and expensive local restaurant. He pulled into the parking lot, turned off the engine, and ran around the car to open my door. He put my arm in his and we walked into the restaurant, acting as mature as we possibly could.

We waited our turn to be seated by the maître d. He looked at us in a way that questioned if we knew how posh and expensive this place was. Just as John began to say we had a reservation, one of the lenses of his glasses popped out and rolled next to the shoe of the maître d, who raised his eyebrows and looked at us with complete disdain.

John made a joke, picked up the lens, and popped it back into his frames, just a little crooked. Pretending that this little incident didn't just happen, we followed the maître d to our table. I looked at the menu and felt nervous about the prices. John noticed and said, "Order whatever you would like. This is our date."

I studied the menu and my eyes landed on "Ribs." I love ribs, but why would I order them on my first date, in my best blue dress, at a classy restaurant? I will never know.

My plate of ribs arrived, smothered in BBQ sauce, and I dug in with both hands. It didn't occur to me to cut the meat off the bone and eat it with a fork. It was delicious and I was a mess. Within minutes, I needed a second white linen napkin, and then a third.

Midway through dinner our server asked, "Is there anything I can get for you?" Bad timing. My teeth were caught in a struggle with a piece of meat that was really stuck to the bone. In an effort to politely answer his question, I yanked at the tough piece of meat. The meat broke free and the bone flew out of my hand, hitting John in the middle of his chest and falling into in his lap.

I was mortified. As John wiped BBQ sauce off of his Sunday tie, the server lost his hold on formality and laughed uncontrollably. Nothing quite like a first date. Somehow we made it through dessert without any more embarrassing moments.

I had to be home by midnight. John turned off the engine and the headlights of the car, coasting into my driveway just before midnight. He reached over and took my hand, pulling me toward him. I looked at his blue eyes as he came close to me, wondering what it would feel like to kiss him.

He kissed me then pulled back to look into my eyes. "I'm going to miss you," he said. His kiss was soft and interesting, but it didn't excite me like I thought it should. It was as if I were observing the kiss, not feeling it. It was okay, I could do it again, but that was about it.

John and I continued to spend a lot of time together. A few weeks before he left on his mission to Argentina, he snuck up behind me at church, took me by the arm, and said, "Hurry, get in the car."

Always up for an adventure, I asked, "Where are we going?"

"Wait and see," he answered. The excitement of the moment overcame my fear that my parents would find out.

John turned off Highway 68 and drove up the canyon. Suddenly, he took a hard turn and went in behind some trees. He said, "Come on, there's a cave up here."

I wondered what was in the cave. In spite of wearing high-heeled shoes, I kept up with John as he climbed the hill. We stepped inside the cave, and he pulled me towards him. He began to kiss me passionately. So much for exploring the cave. I put my arms around John's neck and kissed him back. Eventually, he lay down on the dirt floor of the cave and pulled me on top of him. It was the first time we had been that close.

I felt something stir within me that felt good. "I like this," I thought. "I'm going to miss John." I cared about him, but I noticed I didn't experience that "in love" feeling like I'd seen other girls feel about their boyfriends. I told myself it was too early for those feelings, that we just needed more time together, more practice.

Suddenly he stopped and said, "We'd better leave before we go any further." I agreed, although for me I did not feel remotely like I was headed in that direction, because as much as I enjoyed it, going further was not something my commitment to virginity would let happen. Mormons do not have sex before being married in the temple.

As we left the cave, I looked down at my dress. It was dirty and wrinkled. John's suit was filthy. We quickly brushed each other off, jumped in the car, and went back to church. If anyone noticed, they didn't say a word.

Our escapes to the cave continued for the next four Sundays, then they stopped because John was leaving for Argentina in a week. He had been set apart as a missionary by then and couldn't have physical contact with me.

John asked me to write to him while he was on his mission, and I did.

I loved John. We had great fun together and were close friends. Our friendship gave me the courage to share my secret with him.

There on the couch, kissing John, I pulled back and said, "We need to talk." I was terrified to tell him my deepest, darkest secret, but I couldn't carry it alone anymore. It was too heavy.

I said, "I have something really bad to tell you."

He looked concerned and said, "Okay, Marnie, you can tell me anything."

"I think something is very wrong with me because I have feelings for other girls," I said.

As soon as the words left my mouth, I burst into tears. I had never spoken the words out loud, and hearing myself say them sent me into the deepest, most gut-wrenching cry of my life.

So much was at stake. The only thing louder than my sobs was the screaming voice in my head telling me I had just ruined my life, not to mention John's love for me. Between breaths I assured him I loved him, and I meant it.

John put his arms around me and held me for what seemed like hours. When I finally lifted my head off his chest, I felt too ashamed to look into his eyes.

As I was crying, John did his best to comfort me, but what do you say to a girl you are kissing who has just told you she really likes you but has feelings for other girls, too?

John was older than I, so I looked to him for an answer. I asked, "What should I do?"

He thought for a minute and then said, "You've got to fast, pray, read the Scriptures, and never give in to your feelings." He added, "You also need to read President Kimball's 's book called, *The Miracle of Forgiveness.* It has chapters on homosexuality."

I had been fasting and praying about this for years and had never acted on my feelings, but I could not wait to read the book. I was sure it would have an answer to my "problem."

We said goodnight, and I went up to my room and cried myself to sleep. Surely, I was the most sinful person alive, and certainly I was the only Mormon with this problem.

I took John's suggestion and read *The Miracle of Forgiveness.* If he believed it would help me, I believed it would, too. But reading the book did not offer a solution to my problem; instead, it deepened my shame.

In the chapter, *Crime Against Nature - Sin of the Ages,* I read: "Homosexuality is an ugly sin, repugnant to those who find no temptation in it...." "This perversion is defined as sexual desire for those of the same sex or sexual relations between individuals of the same sex, whether men or women. It is a sin of the ages."

It goes on, "Thus it is that through the ages, perhaps as an extension of homosexual practices, men and women have sunk even to seeking sexual satisfaction with animals. All such deviations from normal, proper heterosexual relationships are not merely unnatural but wrong in the sight of God. Like adultery, incest, and bestiality they carried the death penalty under the

Mosaic law."[1]

Telling John my secret that night gave me little relief, and *The Miracle of Forgiveness* convinced me I was a perversion in God's eyes and that I would be cast into outer darkness if I did not fix whatever was so deeply wrong inside of me.

---

[1] Spencer W. Kimball, "The Miracle of Forgiveness" (Salt Lake City, UT: Publishers Press, 29th Printing, 1997), page 78-79.

Chapter 2
Before "The Secret"

I lived twelve happy years without the dread that I was a homosexual.

I was the oldest of six children, born to parents whose parents and grandparents were Mormon. In fact, my great-great-great grandfather crossed the plains with Brigham Young. My father was a leader in the church, and our family was picture perfect in its rigorous and genuine devotion to it.

When you are born into a committed Mormon family, you become a member of an amazing community of care and instruction. Your path is laid out before you, and all you need to do is follow it to your dream of a happy life here and on the other side. No need to question, just learn obedience, follow the principles, and become a worthy member of The Church of Jesus Christ of Latter Day Saints.

At 3, I became a Sunbeam, which was the first level of what's called "Primary." Once a week, we were taught to be obedient, kind, and in service to others. The song "Popcorn Popping on the Apricot Tree" was a favorite. We lived in Moline, Illinois, and my mom was pregnant with my sister.

In addition to my once-a-week Sunbeam class, we had "Family Home Evening" on Monday nights. Sunday mornings were for Sunday School, followed by a delicious meal at home, then quiet games until we returned in the late afternoon for the Sacrament Meeting. Sundays were Sabbath, which meant wearing dresses all day, no rough housing, and no riding bikes or any other physical activities.

Primary was organized in 1878 by a woman concerned that young Mormon children had too much time on their hands. Their fathers and older brothers were working the fields and the mothers and older sisters were busy cooking and cleaning. In addition to faith, manners, and obedience, boys were taught not to steal fruit from orchards, and girls were taught not to hang on wagons.

After my sister was born, we moved to Bountiful, Utah. My mom's parents lived about a mile from us. My grandmother Josephine was an herbalist and an accomplished gardener. I was crazy about her. She would take me into the mountains to pick wild flowers and huckleberries for her coveted huckleberry jam. Time with my grandmother was the beginning of my love for herbs and natural healing.

It was in Bountiful, at age 4, that I entered kindergarten. I insisted on walking to school by myself. Unbeknownst to me, my mother ran from bush to bush, carrying my baby sister and dragging my little brother by the hand, to be sure I got to school safely. As I was preparing to dash to the other side of a busy four-lane street, a man in a uniform approached me and said he was Mr. Day and his job was to help me cross the street safely. I didn't really want his help but agreed to it when he said the school had a rule about it. I was a Sunbeam after all. I understood rules.

I hated wearing dresses to school, and my shiny Sunday shoes just didn't work on the playground. I wore shorts under my dresses but managing that extra fabric on the monkey bars was a bother. I nagged Mom into a compromise on the shoes. She let me wear my red Keds™ with the white rubber toe instead of my Sunday shoes. More and more, she let me out the door without a dress over my shorts.

When I was 7, we moved to Mendon, Utah, a small town of 650 people in the Rocky Mountains. Still in Primary, the focus was on Obedience: Obedience to our Bishop, to our church leaders and teachers, and to our parents. We were taught the importance of honesty, integrity, kindness, service and following the commandments.

At age eight, my dad baptized me into the Church. This is an important milestone in the life of a Mormon child. My grandparents and some of my aunts and uncles were there to witness my baptism and to see me receive my CTR ring. CTR is an acronym for "Choose The Right." From that moment on, I was to stop before making a decision and choose the right. Based on what I had been taught at church, I knew the difference between right and wrong choices, and at age 8, I was considered old enough to have sins in the eyes of God.

We wore the rings at all times, or more honestly, until we lost them. We were only eight. Truth is, even when the ring wasn't on my finger, it felt like it was.

My eighth birthday was important for another reason. Mom agreed to stop ratting and spraying my hair on Sundays, and I received the harness boots I had been wanting so badly. They were black cowboy boots with a square toe and harness buckles on each side. In order to stop my Sunday morning tears, Mom agreed to let me wear my new boots with my Sunday dress. Sundays became a lot easier for both of us then.

There in Mendon, I met my best-ever friend, Kate. I was the tallest girl in our class and Kate was the shortest. She had long curly blond hair, blue eyes, dimples, and a laugh that made the rest of us laugh, too. Everybody wanted to be Kate's best friend; somehow she chose me. We were inseparable. We played together after school and had sleepovers once a week.

Kate had a younger brother named George. He was my brother's age, and they became best friends, too. The four of us built a clubhouse in one of the old barns on the property next door. Every day after school we played in our clubhouse.

All in all, I was a happy girl living a safe, fun-loving life in a Mormon universe. All needs met. All plans set. I was four years away from hearing the word, *homosexual.* There was still plenty of time for me to feel good about myself and my life.

Chapter 3
Impressing Jenny

My favorite babysitter of all time was Jenny Barker. I was eight years old when she came to babysit for the first time. She was fifteen, had light brown hair, green-blue eyes, and a really big smile, not to mention her groovy bell-bottom blue jeans. I liked her immediately and wanted her to like me.

My mom brought my brother and me into the kitchen to go over the rules we were to follow while she and Dad were gone. I kept glancing over at Jenny as Mom talked. She smiled and gave me a little wink. I liked her even more.

As my parents drove off, I was already coming up with ways to impress Jenny. First, I got on my bike and road as fast as my little legs could pedal. No response.

Next, I got on the swing and pumped until I could not swing any higher. Jenny was holding the hands of my two little sisters while she walked toward the swings. When I got to the highest point of my arc, I let go and sailed through the air. I heard a small gasp from Jenny. Still, not much of a reaction. I was going to have to get creative.

In our front yard there was an enormous tree that my brother and I climbed all the time. So, I tapped him on the shoulder and ran for the tree. He was right behind me. We were in a race, climbing up the tree as fast as we could. I saw Jenny watching us from the corner of her eye. Good. We had her attention.

Soon, she was standing under the tree asking how high we were going to climb. I looked at my brother and said, "Maybe we should hang out on that limb and drop." In an instant, he shimmied across the limb and hung there. I couldn't believe he really did it, and of course, I quickly joined him.

Jenny yelled for us to get down from the tree as she frantically ran back and forth below. I can imagine now what it must have looked like for a six-year old and an eight-year old to be hanging side by side midway up a tall tree with our hands holding tightly to a branch. I was just starting to think we were a little too high to drop when my brother gave me "the look" and let go. Jenny screamed. Of course, I let go, too.

I was pretty sure we had impressed her. We landed in a heap on the ground, the impact too great to stay on our feet. Shaken, I rolled over and looked at my brother to make sure he was okay. He smiled. Jenny helped us up from the ground, brushed us off, and suggested we find something else to do. She looked at me sideways and gave me a grin. Success felt sweet.

My parents went on a date every weekend and Jenny became my favorite babysitter.

A couple of years went by and I no longer did daring feats to impress Jenny. Instead, I began helping her with the kids, and she let me stay up after she put the others to bed. We would often watch TV or eat snacks and talk. I don't remember what we talked about, but I do remember the warmth I felt when she looked into my eyes, smiled, and did a little giggle. For me, that kind of eye connection is like a moment in time where everything stops and all you see is that person.

Chapter 4
Playboys and Candace

My brother, Rohn, and Kate and her brother, George, and I liked to ride our bikes to the bottom of town and put pennies on the railroad tracks. We were headed down there one really cold day when we came upon several dead cows by the track. They were completely frozen after having been hit by the train a couple of days before. The scene was surreal.

George motioned for us to follow him as he ran up and over the bodies of the cows, as if they were big frozen fat logs. I felt nervous as I ran over the first cow. Even though it was dead, I felt bad for the cow, and I was worried something might come out of its mouth. I looked back, the cow didn't move; it was frozen solid. Soon I was running as fast as I could over each cow, never looking back. Running on the cows took us down the tracks further than usual, and we stopped to catch our breath.

Nearby, we noticed pieces of magazines strewn across the tracks, *Playboy* magazines. Our brothers looked at the photos, but Kate and I were not nearly as interested. In fact, I found them nasty and gross. I remember wondering why there were no photos of naked men. From everything we had been taught at church, I knew we should not be looking at these photos. What we were doing was wrong. Even though my CTR ring was long since lost, I still had the habit of looking down at my finger. It was almost like a scar had burned into the skin where my CTR ring once was.

Kate had an older sister, Candace. Many of the boys in our

town had a crush on Candace. She had long brown hair, hazel brown eyes, stylish clothes, and she knew how to dance. Candace always seemed a little bit cranky. Sometimes the boys would chase her, then catch and kiss her. She pretended to put up a little fight, but as I watched the game I could tell she liked it.

One day Kate, George, my brother, and I went to the neighbor's cow corral for a little fun. The idea was to outrun the mother cows when they chased us to protect their calves. The four of us lined up outside the fence. One by one, we would climb up over the fence, run through a hill-sized pile of poop and to the other side of the corral, then jump up and over the opposite fence. Success was all about timing and speed.

On this particular day, Kate, my brother and I had made it across. We yelled at George to get going. As he ran across the corral, a cow was gaining on him. We yelled for him to run faster. George made the mistake of turning to look behind him, which slowed him down just enough for the cow to catch up with him and butt him over the fence. He landed on his rear and was crying as we brought him home.

While George's mom was comforting him inside the house, Candace came outside, mad. She gave Kate and me a piece of her mind. I remember watching her, being so intrigued by her anger.

A couple of days later, we were all playing "Chase." Candace was playing, too. There were barns, haystacks, cow pens, and farm equipment to run over and through. I was "It." The group split off and climbed a haystack, but Candace kept running. I caught up with her, tackled her to the ground, and climbed on top of her.

She tried to get away, but I had her pinned. I looked at her and for the first time wondered what it would be like to kiss her like the boys did. I had thought Candace was cute, but I hadn't thought of kissing her before. I immediately rolled off of her, declared her "It," and went back to playing the game. However, it was hard for me to get Candace out of my mind.

I was ten, now a "Merry Miss" in Primary. As a Merry Miss, I received a long cloth banner imprinted with the thirteen Articles of Faith, which are the center of the core beliefs in the Mormon Church, that generations of Merry Misses before me had also memorized. It had a pocket at the top where a dowel would be inserted so we could display our work once it was completed.

We would not only memorize and discuss each of the Articles, we would cross-stitch a beautiful design at the top. As we memorized and stitched each Article of Faith, we were rewarded with an emblem to glue onto the banner.

The Articles of Faith:

1. *We believe in God, the Eternal Father, and in His Son, Jesus Christ, and in the Holy Ghost.*

2. *We believe that men will be punished for their own sins, and not for Adam's transgression.*

3. *We believe that through the Atonement of Christ, all mankind may be saved, by obedience to the laws and ordinances of the Gospel.*

4. *We believe that the first principles of ordinances of the Gospel are: first, Faith in the Lord Jesus Christ; second, Repentance; third, Baptism by immersion for the remission of sins; fourth, Laying on of hands for the gift of the Holy Ghost.*

5. *We believe that a man must be called of God, by prophecy, and by the laying on of hands by those who are in authority, to preach the Gospel and administer in the ordinances thereof.*

6. *We believe in the same organization that existed in the Primitive Church, namely, apostles, prophets, pastors, teachers, evangelists, and so forth.*

7. *We believe in the gift of tongues, prophecy, revelation, visions, healing, interpretation of tongues, and so forth.*

8. *We believe the Bible to be the word of God as afar as it is translat-*

ed correctly; we also believe the Book of Mormon to be the word of God.

9. *We believe all that God has revealed, all that He does now reveal, and we believe that He will yet reveal many great and important things pertaining to the Kingdom of God.*

10. *We believe in the literal gathering of Israel and in the restoration of the Ten Tribes; that Zion (the New Jerusalem) will be built upon the American continent; that Christ will reign personally upon the earth; and, that the earth will be renewed and receive its paradisiacal glory.*

11. *We claim the privilege of worshiping Almighty God according to the dictates of our own conscience, and allow all men the same privilege, let them worship how, where, or what they may.*

12. *We believe in being subject to kings, presidents, rulers, and magistrates, in obeying, honoring and sustaining the law.*

13. *We believe in being honest, true, chaste, benevolent, virtuous, and in doing good to all men; indeed, we may say that we follow the admonition of Paul - We believe all things, we hope all things, we have endured many things, and hope to be able to endure all things. If there is anything virtuous, lovely or of good report or praiseworthy, we seek after these things.*

I completed my assignment as a Merry Miss, the Articles of Faith stitched on my banner and my heart. Little did I know that I was approaching the end of my innocent, carefree life, and that this would be the end of my feeling "normal" like the other kids.

Chapter 5
I Turn Twelve

My twelfth year brought three changes to my life: a move to Idaho, a church graduation, and a class that would shift me forever. I welcomed my church graduation, but the other two caught me completely off guard.

The first change that rattled me was a move from Mendon, Utah, to Idaho Falls, Idaho. Dad's work as a pioneer in roller coaster design and ski chair lift design required us to move more often than any of us liked. This one came without much notice. I was heartbroken. Life was so fun in Mendon. My best friend in the world was there, not to mention farm life, the clubhouse, and the crazy games we played.

One advantage of being a member of the Mormon Church is that wherever you move there is a community of like-minded friends waiting for you. You are immediately brought into church life and service activities. Except for the scenery and the people, our family of eight didn't miss a beat in this new town. Same teachings, same schedules, same rules, same expectations. However, I missed Kate terribly.

I made the school basketball team. I loved being on a team. We played hard, worked hard, looked out for each other, and learned how to win and how to lose. We practiced five days a week, and I made friends with the other players, which took the edge off of my loneliness for Kate, who I spoke with as often as possible by phone.

Basketball saved me in my seventh grade year.

I Turn Twelve

At church I was excited to graduate from Primary to Mutual - *Mutual Improvement Association* - which later became *Young Women's and Young Men's.* These were church classes and activities for 12-17 year-olds. I was finally old enough to join the teenagers.

Mutual was divided by age groups. The first two years were Beehive, the second two were Mia Maid, and the last two were Laurel. Each year, there would be a spiritual focus to understand and achieve. As a new inductee into the Beehives, I was immersed into a focus on strengthening faith in Heavenly Father and Jesus Christ, learning to work with others in harmony and cooperation, stand for truth and righteousness, and learn leadership.

The idea for a youth association was advised by church founder, Joseph Smith, in 1843. It was first called, "*The Young Ladies' Department of the Cooperative Retrenchment Association.*" Joseph Smith declared this vision for the young women of the church: "I desire them to retrench from extravagance in dress, in eating and even in speech. The time has come when the sisters must agree...to set an example worthy of imitation before the people of the world...There is need for the young daughters of Israel to get a living testimony of the truth...We are about to organize a Retrenchment Association, which I want you all to join, and I want you to vote to retrench in everything that is not good and beautiful, not to make yourselves unhappy, but to live so you may be truly happy in this life and the life to come."

I was onboard.

My friend, Mya, became the Beehive President and I was her First Counselor. We worked with our teacher to plan fun activities, reach out to inactive girls in our ward, and help plan spiritual lessons.

At the same time, I enrolled in a church program called, *Personal Progress*, which was an achievement and goal-setting program to help us know we were daughters of God, rely upon the Holy Ghost, and develop personal religious behaviors, such as prayer, scripture study, obedience to commandments, and service. The program helped us keep our baptismal covenants and prepare and qualify for temple covenants (marriage in the temple), develop talents and skills that prepared us for our future roles, and establish a pattern of step-by-step progress through our lives.

As part of the *Personal Progress* program, I was given a white book with beautiful religious pictures in it. I was to talk with my parents and set personal goals each year, and then convey my goals to my teacher. My white book served as a planning and accountability book for my spiritual growth and goals. All young women were encouraged to do this, so of course, I was all about it.

The third change of my twelfth year occurred during a Mutual class on morality. Most of our classes were with girls our own age. This one involved a special meeting for all the kids, boys and girls, aged 12-17. The Bishop and our individual advisors were also there.

When I entered the chapel with my friends, I was an open-hearted, adventurous girl, the oldest of six children in a devout Mormon family. I enjoyed being with both boys and girls, and was only mildly aware that my enjoyment of girls seemed a little overboard as compared to how other girls felt about girls. The urges were innocent. I was aware but not alarmed.

However, by the time walked out of that room, I was a girl with a dread I had never known. My dread was that I might be what the speaker from Salt Lake City called, "a homosexual," a person who was attracted to people of their same gender. If it was true, I would be banished from the church, not allowed into Heaven, separated from my family forever, not be permitted to marry in the Temple, be cast into outer darkness, and perhaps worst of all, be tried in a Mormon Church Court.

In other words, my life as I knew it and loved it was on the line if I was a homosexual. My gut tightened and I felt like I was going to throw up.

I Turn Twelve

The secret dread that I was homosexual moved in like an unwanted, tormenting roommate, demanding more and more of me. It drove me to work hard to practice the principles of the gospel, while begging God to make me "normal." I vowed to live a perfect Mormon life and prayed fervently to God to take these strange feelings from me. I believed he would. He had to!

I clung to a guarantee a leader in the church from Salt Lake City had made to our youth group, and later to our parents. He said, "If you attend early morning seminary, and fast and pray, I *guarantee* you will grow up and be married in the temple, every single one of you." I believed his promise included me. Surely I could believe him.

So I worked even harder, but my feelings for girls remained.

I assured myself it couldn't be true. I was Marnie Freeman. I loved God. I obeyed the rules of God and the church. I was an obedient child, who took good care of my brothers and sisters, and I was a loyal friend. How could God let me be a homosexual?

He wouldn't. I would pray and obey it away.

Chapter 6
Jollie Holds My Hand

During eighth grade, one night after basketball practice, I was waiting with some of the other players for our parents to pick us up. I was standing at the top of the stairs with my gym bag in one hand when someone took hold of my other hand. I was surprised to see it was Jollie, a teammate. She was squatting down, pretending to be a little kid who needed help walking down the stairs.

I liked holding her hand. When we got to the bottom of the stairs, I thought she would let go, but she didn't. We walked through the halls, holding hands. She was one of the cutest girls on the team. So much so that I wished I hadn't called my mom to come pick me up.

As Mom pulled up in front of the school, I said goodbye to Jollie and let go of her hand. I wondered if I would ever hold her hand again. To my delight, we played the same game after practice the following night. Again, I wished I could hold her hand longer. But it was the last time we played the game.

There was a boy I often sat next to on the bus. Sometimes we held hands, too. Holding hands with Jollie was different, a difference I not only noticed, but couldn't exactly define. I was worried.

Was this normal? Did it mean I was a homosexual? I couldn't ask. It had to remain a secret.

Chapter 7
Worse Than a Terrorist

In the middle of my eighth grade year, our parents called a family meeting to tell us that Dad had a job opportunity in California. They asked us to vote whether or not he should take it. At first we were excited. Then we kids decided we liked it in Idaho Falls. The vote was to stay put. I was relieved. We had lived there a year and a half, and I didn't want to move again.

A few weeks later, while watching the kids when my parents were out, someone called to ask if the snowmobile was still for sale. I cringed because I knew the only reason we would ever sell it was if we were going to move. Sure enough, my parents had decided to relocate us to California in spite of the family vote.

How could they do this? I was in the middle of a great year. I was on a great basketball team, liked my teammates and coach, and didn't want to leave our church. I liked the kids and my Mutual teacher. My brothers and sisters didn't want to move either. But the decision had been made, and we moved to Salinas, California.

Salinas is a beautiful town off the coast of California, near Monterey and Carmel. Once again, I adjusted to the new location and returned to the familiar routine of church, school, family, and sports.

Fortunately, we spent Christmases in Utah with my grandparents and extended family, which gave me a chance to be with my beloved friend, Kate, for a couple of days.

One year, I was able to spend an extra three days with Kate, and even go to school with her. I still don't know why, but I got the silly notion to dress up as Mamee from the book, *Little Women.* Before Christmas break, I had made a little movie based on the book for a school project. My friend Stacy had played the role of Mamee, and I still had the black makeup and wig. I took it with me to Utah.

Before Kate and I left for school, I applied the makeup and put on the wig. Kate began to feel a little nervous about the idea. Her mom warned, "I am not going to pick you up if they won't let you go to school." I assured her they would let me go to school. After all, my disguise looked real.

I glanced at myself in the mirror as I left the house, hoping I was right.

We got to school, and everybody was looking at me as Kate and I walked down the hall. I started to feel a little self-conscious and wondered if I had made a good choice.

The bell rang as we sat down in Kate's first class. The teacher took roll, put down his pencil and then walked toward the back of the classroom, looking at me. I kept my eyes down. He stopped and tapped his finger on my desk. I looked up at him with my eyes, trying not to raise my head. I figured as little exposure as possible was a good idea at this point.

The teacher told me to go to the principal's office. As I stood up, I looked over at Kate. Her head was in her hands. She was trying not to laugh as I followed the teacher out of the room and down to the principal's office.

As we walked into the administrative office, everyone stopped working to look at me. I sank into a seat and didn't move. After a few minutes, a nice lady led me into the office where the principal was waiting. I sat in the chair, not sure where to look.

He stared at me with laser-like eyes, then leaned forward and said with a country accent, "What do you think you're doin' comin' into my school dressed like that? I don't know if you're a criminal, if you're on the run, or what you might be."

I felt my eyes widen as I looked at him. Could he have me arrested? He continued on. The longer he talked, the louder he spoke.

Finally, he said, "You need to go home." I was relieved. No sheriff.

Then he leaned way back in his chair, put his cowboy boots up on the desk, and clasped his hands over his large belly. As I got up to go, he said, "Hell, comin' to my school incognito, for all I know you could be a terrorist - or a homosexual for that matter!"

His comment shook me to the core. Being a homosexual is as bad, or worse, than being a terrorist? Could he have sensed something about me that had made him say that?

Kate's sister, Candace, drove us home. She was not pleased. "How could you do something so stupid? Who thought of such a dumb idea? How could you think they would let you stay at school?"

Good friend that she was, Kate never gave me up.

Still, I had bigger worries than Candace's anger. How could being a homosexual be worse than being a terrorist?! It was clear to me that something about me had made the principal think I was a homosexual. Granted, with my makeup and wig, I did look like the main star in the "Rocky Horror Picture Show."

Chapter 8
My Attraction Increases

The principal's words haunted me and fueled a growing concern over my attraction to girls. My feelings were becoming bigger and not going away. There had to be something I could do. I intensified my prayers to Heavenly Father about my feelings for girls. I figured since God knows everything, He already knew about me, so I didn't bother with a lot of explaining. I renewed my standing promise to follow his program as perfectly as I could. I would use my "Fast Sundays" to focus on this one thing and would stop taking shortcuts, like sneaking sips of water when I brushed my teeth. I swore I would be the best Mormon kid I could possibly be if he would just take away my feelings for girls.

I had plenty of opportunities to prove I meant it.

In ninth grade, I began attending early morning seminary. I woke up at 5:15 AM and left my house at 5:45 for a thirty-minute carpool ride to North Salinas with other high school kids from our ward. During the school year, this became our daily routine until we graduated from high school.

The goal of seminary was to become familiar with, and to gain, a personal testimony of the scriptures, *The Book of Mormon, The New Testament, The Old Testament, The Doctrine and Covenants,* and *The Pearl of Great Price.* We were required to read and study each of these texts and to memorize 160 specific scriptures, although we did not have to read the *Old Testament* in its entirety.

At 15, I became Mia Maid President with two counselors and a secretary. I attended early morning seminary each weekday,

Sunday School and Sacrament on Sundays, and a young women's spiritual meeting and activity each week. I had personal prayer each morning and night, prayed at each of my meals (although I admit I skipped praying when I was at school), and I fasted the first Sunday of every month. My family had Family Home Evenings each Monday night, which included a spiritual lesson on three Mondays and a family activity on the fourth Monday. I was working with my *Personal Progress* journal and meeting all of my goals. I did everything I could possibly think of.

In addition to this, I met regularly with my Bishop to answer two questions: Was I a worthy member of the church, and was I a full tithe payer (10% of all income)?

I was a full tither, so that answer came easily. When he asked if I was a worthy member of the church I said *yes,* but felt a knot form in my stomach. I justified that I was still worthy because I had never acted on my feelings. Honestly, I wasn't sure, because I knew homosexuality was one of the worst sins, a sin equal to murder.

Above all, I begged God to take away my growing attraction to girls.

Chapter 9
Just a Normal Kid

I had always been the kid who loved having fun and often instigated memorable adventures. Once I realized my feelings for girls could mean I was a homosexual, I used fun as an escape from dread. Having fun forced me to focus on the moment, not on the chatter in my head.

Most weeks after youth group, a bunch of us would head out for hot fudge Sundays at Oscar Hossenfelder's on Cannery Row or an elaborate game of hide and seek. Another one of our favorite games was to crawl or walk along the planks that zigzagged beneath the Monterey Wharf. Often we snuck down one of the ladders to get to the maze of narrow planks below. At night it was pitch black, and we had to use all our senses to follow the thin path of planks in the dark. Slowly, we would place one foot in front of the other, hoping not to misjudge the path and fall into the Bay.

One moonless night, I was the leader and my brother and several of our friends were walking behind me. We were deep under the wharf, and I could not see a thing. Our nervous breathing blocked out the sounds coming from the restaurants above. In some places, the planks widened into 6' x 8' docking areas to accommodate the rowboats that had been used during the time when the canneries were still in operation. Now, instead of rowboats, huge sea lions would often sleep there. Seeing the mammoth creatures sprawled out in front of us added a little more challenge and excitement to our game.

I continued down the dark planks, placing one foot slowly in front of the other, sometimes tapping on the boards with my toe to make sure I was still on the plank and that there wasn't a turn in the path or a sleeping sea lion.

You know how the movie *Friday the Thirteenth* ends with the one surviving girl floating peacefully in a canoe on the lake and you feel so relieved that she is safe and the movie is over? Then, all of a sudden, Jason comes out of the water and grabs her from behind to the sound of screeching music?

Well, there on the planks that dark night, the water was completely still and quiet. Suddenly I felt a huge snort of air come at me as an enormous sea lion shot up out of the ocean, landing all of its 600 pounds onto the dock, missing me by inches.

We all jumped and screamed and somehow kept our balance. It still gives me the shivers and makes me laugh.

On another night after youth group, we went over to Cannery Row. I'm pretty good at finding ways into closed buildings, which meant I occasionally led some pretty great expeditions inside the old, vacant canneries. No, I wasn't a thief or a vandal, just a curious kid who liked harmless challenges and excitement. At the time, if you drove down Cannery Row, it looked like a line of solid, closed up canneries and buildings. Most of these were false facings, but you only knew that if you could get in behind them.

I led the group over a cement barricade and down to the water. As before, we walked silently under the structure supporting the canneries above, which was very similar to our times at the wharf. There were cement chutes along the way which the cannery workers had used to send the fish guts back into the bay.

We climbed up one of the chutes and landed in a huge, dilapidated cannery. Most of the ceiling had fallen into the water, and there were square rooms filled with empty sardine cans and sardine labels, worthless then and very valuable now. We wound our way up, down, over, and through several canneries, eventually coming to a tall fence with menacing barbed wire at the top.

Looking through the fence, I could see the famous Doc Ricketts lab that John Steinbeck had written about in many of his novels. I had read many of Steinbeck's books in my American Lit. class, and I had loved when he talked about Doc Ricketts.

With a little balancing and a lot of dare, we shimmied to the other side of the fence by hanging out over the water. Doc Ricketts' lab was completely dark. We walked around the cement specimen tanks, hoping to find something interesting. Unfortunately, the tanks were empty. Even so, it was great to be in the actual lab of Doc Ricketts.

We climbed out of the lab and into the second story of a huge warehouse. A light was on in a room on the main floor, and we realized someone was in there, working. So we tiptoed our way through hundreds of amazing wharf memorabilia - weathered wooden figureheads from the prow of old ships, statues of mermaids covered in green moss, old pirates with limbs missing, and big wooden treasure chests. It felt as if we were walking along the ocean floor. Being good Mormon kids, we never destroyed or took anything.

Suddenly, a man said "Hey, who's in here?"

I whispered, "Everybody hide!"

Our friend Brent, not thinking ahead about the possible need to run, crawled into a big chest and closed the lid. I hid behind a statue and watched as the guy searched for us. I wanted to tell everyone to run but I didn't want to leave Brent in the chest, so we waited, hoping to remain unseen.

The guy searched for us without luck, and then he saw the chest. I watched as he walked toward it and slowly lifted the lid. There was Brent scrunched in a ball on his side, not daring to breathe.

"What are you doing in here?" The guy was as puzzled as he was upset.

I came out from behind the statue and said, "We were just playing hide and seek." The other kids slowly emerged, surprising the guy even more. He told us to get out of there and never come back. Sheepishly, we complied.

The intensity of these adventures gave me a few hours' relief from the constant ache in my gut, and just for a moment, I could be a normal kid.

Chapter 10
While John Was In Argentina

I was now sixteen, and John was on his mission in Argentina. The trips to the caves were a recent memory. Before he left, I wondered how I would feel when he was gone. I deeply missed my friend, but I was not as heartbroken as I thought a girlfriend should be.

One night after youth group, we all decided to go swimming at the condo clubhouse of one of the kids. It was after hours, so we snuck in quietly. I was in the first car to arrive and changed quickly into my swim suit.

As I was walking over to the hot tub, a girl from Carmel took me by the arm and asked me to follow her. She was one of the most beautiful girls in our ward, but I didn't know her very well. She led me back into a fenced area where we were alone.

I looked at her and said, "Yeah?"

I noticed her long, dark hair, her olive skin, sparkling green eyes, and perfectly white teeth. My eyes glanced at her slender body in her light green bathing suit.

She looked into my eyes and stepped toward me. In an instant, I faced a choice I couldn't believe. Should I move toward her and follow my urge to know the feel of her lips on mine, or should I resist?

I heard another car pull up and kids laughing as they got out of the cars. I looked at the girl in front of me for a split second and said, "Come on. Everybody's here."

I turned and left, hardly able to breathe. We never spoke of it and acted as if it had never happened. But the experience brought me face to face with my feelings. I adored John. I loved what I felt toward him, but all my time with John did not begin to make me feel like that one second of facing the girl in the green suit. That split second touched the depths of my very being.

During the day I could stop myself from thinking of her, but at night when I tried to fall asleep, I could see her standing in front of me. As hard as I tried, I could not get her out of my mind. I tossed and turned as I asked God to help me. He didn't seem to be listening.

A month later, I was at my weekly youth group meeting. This meeting was in the chapel and included both boys and girls. A special speaker was talking on the topic of morality, a common theme.

Initially, he spoke of temple marriage and the absolute necessity of waiting to have intercourse until after marriage. He continued onto other things I had heard many times, and then he paused.

When he began talking again, he turned the subject to homosexuality. It caught me off-guard. No teacher had mentioned the word since that meeting when I'd first heard it when I was twelve. My ears felt hot as I nervously looked down at the pew in front of me. I stared at a songbook, trying not to breathe or move.

I had that sick feeling of heaviness that comes over your entire body when you've done something wrong. I hated the sound of that word, *homosexual.* When I heard the word at age twelve, I worried that I might be homosexual. Now, five years later, I was pretty certain I was.

I felt absolutely sick. How could I possibly be a homosexual?

A week later, while sitting in church, I thought of an idea. I would have a secret end-all goal for my *Personal Progress* book. I wouldn't tell a single person, but every goal I set would help me return to being normal, to not be *that.*

I continued believing if I fasted, prayed and was consistent and worked hard enough, all of these feelings would go away. They had to. After all, that speaker from Salt Lake had guaranteed it.

Chapter 11
Girls' Choice Dance

It had been over a year and John was still in Argentina. We wrote every week, but my feelings had not changed. I loved John; I felt like he was my confidant, and my best friend, but I didn't have that "in love" feeling. I was sure there had to be something more. Although I was in crisis on the inside, I kept my life looking normal on the outside, which included dating and even kissing my dates. It was fun and I enjoyed it, but something was missing.

My friends Lisa and Gwen talked me into going to the Girls' Choice dance together. We decided on the guys we wanted to invite and what our plan would be. Of course, we had to do something a little crazy.

I invited Morgan to be my date with a poem written with a candy bar theme. My mom helped me write the poem using as many candy bar names as we could think of. I took a large poster board, wrote the poem, and taped the candy bars in the appropriate places. Morgan said, 'Yes.' We had dated several times and were great friends. Nothing serious. Lisa had dated Dustin since her freshman year so she invited him. Gwen asked our friend Perry.

On the day of the dance, we arranged to borrow my dad's gold station wagon. Lisa and Gwen came over after breakfast to wash and shine it inside and out. Then we wrote "Just Married" on the windows and attached strings of cans and shoes from the back bumper. We laughed hysterically as we put on the finishing touches. We couldn't wait to pick up the boys.

As the three of us got in the car, the neighbors in our cul-de-sac popped out of their houses to see what the racket was all about. They happily waved us on our way, and we sped off to get the guys.

The looks on the boys' faces proved our plan had worked. We drove to the Rocky Point Restaurant where we'd made reservations. The restaurant was perched on the edge of a cliff in Big Sur. As I looked around I saw dark wooden panels, crisp linen table cloths, crystal wine glasses, candle light, and twinkling lights that created a soft warm glow on the windows. I looked at the fiery sun setting on the horizon, thinking this experience should feel special and amazing. Instead, I felt uncomfortable and unsettled inside. After dinner, we headed for the dance.

The idea of dancing only with Morgan all evening seemed awkward to me, even boring. We were great friends but I couldn't imagine dancing with him the entire night. When *Stairway to Heaven* came on - the longest slow song of all time - Morgan pulled me closer. I wondered how I was going to make it through. I looked around the darkened room at the other couples. Some were making out, appearing to really enjoy themselves. My mind wandered to the trips to the caves with John, then to the girl in the green bathing suit.

I looked over at Lisa and Dustin. They were dancing really close. I realized I would rather be dancing with her. The idea didn't shock me, but I didn't expect it. I froze in place. Morgan tripped over my foot. I pulled myself together and we continued, but the door had opened. I wanted to dance with Lisa more than with Morgan.

We went to a friend's house after the dance to hang out and eat. I made a lame attempt at conversation with Morgan, forcing myself to have fun, lighten up and joke around, but it didn't work. I felt like I was drinking flat 7-Up.

Then Lisa took my arm and said, "Come on." As I followed her upstairs, she said, "Let's go have a nap."

It seemed odd to leave our dates downstairs while we took a nap, but I didn't resist. Earlier, we had changed into shorts and flip-flops, so Lisa kicked off her flip-flops, pulled back the covers of somebody's bed and jumped in. Nervously, I slid in beside her.

We talked and giggled for a while and then she closed her eyes and drifted off to sleep. I laid there watching her, listening to her soft breath. I was so confused. I wasn't in love with her; I didn't even necessarily want to be there with her. But I realized I felt more for her than any of the guys I was dating.

With guys I had fun, and sometimes it became physical. I could be attracted, but something was missing. With girls, though, I felt something different; I came alive in a way I hadn't felt before - electric, excited, and breathless, like the sun coming out on a gray day or the blooming of a brilliant flower.

Morgan kissed me when I dropped him off that night. I felt nothing.

Chapter 12
I Tell My Teacher and Bishop

By the time John returned from Argentina, two years had passed and I was in my senior year. I knew I cared for him, even loved him. I also knew my feelings for him were not as deep or exciting as the feelings I had experienced with the few girls who had taken my breath away by just being near them.

I had come to believe that I was a homosexual, a lesbian, and I had to find a way not to be one. I would do anything because my entire existence depended on it. John was someone I could trust, and I knew he loved me enough to help me overcome it.

On the night I told John my secret, as he held me in his strong arms, he suggested I tell my Mutual teacher. I promised him I would.

Two weeks passed before I mustered up the courage to do it. I just couldn't carry the burden alone anymore. I needed help. One night after Mutual, my teacher drove me home. I think she could sense I wanted to talk because she began sharing secrets about herself as a teenager. There was an easy camaraderie between us, even though she was married and had children.

I listened to her tell me about her experiences as a teenager, knowing that what I was about to tell her would not be the kind of secret she would expect me to share. My heart pounded in my ears as I waited to speak.

I finally said, "I have a secret I need help with and I don't know where to turn." My teacher became quiet, like you do when someone's about to tell you something important.

"I have feelings for girls," I said. "I have tried to feel differently, and I've worked hard for God's help, but the feelings won't go away."

I saw shock in her eyes, the kind of shock that says you have just moved from "great" to "awful" in that person's opinion. Our cozy chat was over; she was about to call in the big guns.

With chilling formality, she said, "Marnie, promise me you will walk into your house and go straight to the phone to call Bishop Roberts tonight. You need to talk to him right away." I promised her I would do it, and I did.

A groggy voice answered the phone. It was after 11:00 P.M. I told Bishop Roberts I had to talk with him immediately. He said, "Tonight? Do you really need to talk with me tonight?"

I was surprised by his hesitation. I had been taught the Bishop was there for you whenever you needed him. He definitely did not want to meet that night. I was tempted to agree to meet at another time, but I had made a promise. With resignation, he told me to come over to his house.

Little did I know this would be one of the most humiliating experiences of my entire life!

I was a nervous wreck as I drove the ten minutes to his house. Pulling into the driveway, I felt like throwing up. Terror filled my heart as I walked to the front door.

I could see one small light on in the house. Maybe he had gone back to bed, thinking my call was just a bad dream. I tried to swallow the lump in my throat before knocking, secretly hoping he wouldn't hear me. I turned to go, then the door slowly opened. The handsome Bishop's hair was disheveled, and he was wearing a bathrobe.

"Hi Bishop," I said. He motioned me to follow him back to his study where I sat down in a chair across from his desk.

"What is so important that you needed to see me tonight?" he asked.

My jaw felt frozen shut, making my words come out in slow motion. "My Mutual teacher told me to do it. She believes you can help me," I said.

"Help you with what?" he asked.

I took a deep breath and said, "I am attracted to girls."

Did he almost fall out of his chair, or did we have a slight earthquake?

The Bishop looked at me with disgust. "I am shocked," he said. "Of all the youth in our stake, you are the last I would expect to tell me this. You are a leader, and all the other kids look up to you. How could you even think to act in such a foul, unnatural way?!"

I told him I had not ever acted on my feelings, but that I had felt this way for a long time. I couldn't bear to see the disappointment and judgment in his eyes and began to reassure him about how much I liked boys and didn't want these strange, unnatural feelings toward girls.

"I will do anything to change the way I feel," I said, "I will do whatever you or the church leaders think I need to do. Anything!"

The more I tried to explain, the more disapproving he became.

He said, "The feelings you have are completely unnatural and ungodly. If you want to spend eternity with your family, you can never act on them."

Then he said, "If you were to be hung on a cross, you would belong between a murderer and a pedophile."

Tears filled my eyes, but I bit my lip so I wouldn't cry. I didn't want him to see the pain I felt in my heart. He stood up, and I knew it was time for me to leave.

"I need to speak with the Stake President because of the seriousness of your problem," he said. "Call me in a few days. We will need to meet on a regular basis."

"I will," I said. "Thank you for seeing me at such a late hour." I went to hug him goodbye, but he sidestepped to avoid it and used his arm to lead me to the door.

"Just make it to the car," I repeated to myself as I walked to my car.

I got in the car and couldn't seem to remember which way was reverse. Luckily, I released the brake and the car rolled back down the driveway. I put the car in first gear and drove away. When I reached the highway, I could no longer control my sobs. It was raining hard outside, and between the tears and the rain blocking my vision, I am amazed I made it home safely.

I stayed in the car for a long while until my crying subsided, then quietly let myself into the house and slipped into bed. A light was on in my parent's room, so I knew my Mom was waiting up for me. I pulled the covers over my head, hoping she would not make me come talk with her. Thankfully, she didn't.

I called Bishop Roberts three days later. He asked me to come to his office. I was terrified I was going to be ex-communicated from the church and put through church court because of the sinful feelings in my heart. My guilt was huge, and I believed I deserved whatever consequences came to me, even though I had never acted on my feelings.

I met with the Bishop early that evening. He said, "I have spoken with the Stake President."

In the Mormon Church, Bishops reign over the local congregations, called Wards. There are usually five to eight wards per Stake. Stake Presidents oversee all the Bishops and their Wards. The Stake President and his High Council have offices in the Stake House, which is much larger than a regular church.

As the Bishop spoke to me, I thought about how serious this must be for him to have talked to the Stake President about me. The Stake President was the father of one of my best friends, so knowing he knew my secret made it even worse.

"We have decided you need to tell your parents and then together we will choose the best course of action for you," he said.

"I cannot tell my father," I said. I admire my dad and had spent my entire life finding ways to impress him. How could I ever tell him something like this? How could I endure his disappointment?

"I will tell my Mom, but not my Dad," I said. "How would you feel if your daughter had to tell you something like this?"

"Okay," he said, "I guess you can just tell your mother, and we will decide where to go from there."

I was so relieved that I didn't have to tell my father that I forgot for a minute about how terrible it would be to tell my mother.

Bishop Roberts opened a drawer in his desk and pulled out a brochure. He handed it to me and said, "Take this home and read it."

When I got home, I read the brochure. It was titled *To The One*. It began, "Will the 99.9% of you bear with me while I address the .01% of you that have these feelings unbecoming of God?" It got worse from there.

I had never read anything so judgmental and hopeless. As a seventeen-year old teenager, who had never acted on a single feeling, looking to the people I trusted the most for help, I felt like an abomination in the eyes of God. I felt alone and unworthy. Still, I read that brochure over and over and carried it with me for years, reading it each time I felt worthless, as if to prove to myself that I was.

Chapter 13
I Tell My Parents

The Bishop had ordered me to tell my mother. A week went by and I still hadn't talked to her. I pled with God to rid me of my feeling for girls so my parents would never have to know. Each morning that week, I had promised myself that I would talk to my mother that day, but just couldn't do it. I knew she was going to be so sad, so shocked, and so disappointed.

The wait became too much. So, one morning I went down to breakfast and asked Mom for some time to talk that night. With five brothers and sisters, privacy needed to be arranged ahead of time. Dad was on a business trip.

I added, "If you're too busy, it's no problem. We can talk another time."

"No, it will work," she said.

I was a bundle of nerves throughout the day. In the evening, Mom fed the family, cleaned things up, made lunches, and put the younger kids to bed. She literally worked from sun up to sun down. I hoped she would be too tired to talk.

"Okay, Marn, shall we talk now?"

Together, we walked up the stairs to her bedroom. By now, I was familiar with the sick feeling that came along with telling my secret. I felt like I was about to ruin my mother's life. She settled into her blue reading chair, and I sat on her bed.

"Mom, unless you really need to share what I'm going to say to you with Dad, I'd like this to be between the two of us," I said.

"Okay, I won't say anything to him," she said.

I explained that what I had to tell her would be very difficult for her to hear. I apologized for what I had to say, and then I told her.

"I have feelings for other girls," I said.

This time it was Mom's turn to bite her lip to keep from crying. I could see the tears in her eyes, but she did not let them stay. She quickly assumed her role as the "fix-it Mom."

"There has to be an answer out there somewhere, and we just have to find it," she said.

"Do you really think so?" I asked.

I had dealt with my feelings for years and hardly dared believe there could be a way to end them. I trusted my Mom with all my heart, and if she thought there was an answer, I would join her in believing it, too.

"You certainly can't be the first person with this problem," she said.

"Really?" I said. "What about being the first person in the church with this problem?"

"Surely not," she said. "We will search high and low until we find an answer." She tried to be very strong and supportive. She hugged me and told me that she loved me and that we would find the answer together.

For the first time in a long time, I went to bed feeling lighter. Somewhere out there was an answer. We just had to find it. I woke up several times during the night and noticed my Mom's light was still on. I imagined her praying and crying to God with all her might.

As far as I know, my mother didn't share my secret with my father. She met with the Bishop several times over the course of a couple of weeks to formulate a plan. Finally, my mom told me they had found a therapist up near San Francisco who had dealt with "this sort of problem" before.

"Has he had success with other people like me?" I asked.

She said, "Yes, absolutely!"

I was worried. How do you change the way you feel? I wasn't trying to change a habit or an act. I was literally trying to change the feelings in my heart. But I was willing to do anything, whatever they asked. So I agreed to go to the therapist once a week, two hours away.

I knew the time would come to tell my father, and it came before I began my appointments with the therapist in San Francisco. Oddly enough, Dad was perched in the same blue chair my mother was sitting in when I changed her life forever, too.

It was unbearably difficult. I had worked my entire life to make him proud of me, and with one sentence I felt I had torn everything to pieces. I will never forget the look of sadness on his face. As tears rolled down his cheeks, something I had never seen before, he assured me he loved me, and I believed him. Still, I had just changed his life as he knew it, and not for the better.

Chapter 14
My First Therapist

This was a busy time in my life. I had graduated from high school and enrolled at Hartnell Junior College in Salinas. I planned to transfer to a four-year college, but wasn't sure which one it would be. Brigham Young University was my first choice, of course.

I had always played sports, and the basketball coach asked me to play on her team. I needed to do something fun to counteract the ever-present sadness and confusion inside of me. Plus, high school and the good times I'd had with my circle of friends had ended. This left a big hole in my social life that basketball could fill.

I happily told my parents I had signed up for the team. They said I couldn't play, and that I needed to focus on my studies and therapy.

I was disappointed but committed to doing whatever it took to "change." I told the coach I couldn't play after all, and I scheduled my first therapy appointment.

I felt nervous and excited as I drove to meet my therapist for the first time. "He may have the answer to my problem," I thought. I reminded myself that he had a successful track record of changing people like me, and I imagined I was only two hours away from the answer I had begged God for years to find.

I had only seen therapists on television. This would be my first chance to meet one in person. I parked the car and walked up to his office. I filled out some paperwork and waited in the lobby.

What would he look like? How would he feel about me? Would he treat me like Bishop Roberts? I hoped not.

After a short wait, the therapist came to the door and invited me into a room that was arranged for conversation. His name was Fritz. He had dark greying hair, narrow brown eyes, and a quick smile as he sat forward, attentively waiting to listen. He seemed friendly as he asked me to share my story. He even appeared to be listening to me without judgment, which was a huge relief.

When I was finished telling him my story, my heart waited on the edge of its seat to hear the answer that would help me to get over my sinful feelings. I was ready to do whatever it took.

I waited, but nothing came. He didn't suggest a solution or a plan. He just wanted to talk. For the first time, I began to doubt. I doubted the Bishop, my mother, my father, and the therapist. Did any of them really know what they were talking about? Or were they just hoping?

The drive home felt very lonely. The fear that there was no way to get rid of my feelings for girls returned even bigger than before. I realized that this thing would not just go away. It couldn't be fasted away or prayed away or pretended away into something it was not. Hard work or high hopes were not going to change my feelings or who I was.

Still, the next week, I returned for my second visit with Fritz. I was willing to give it another try, meaning I was unwilling to completely give up hope. Plus, I had a question I wanted to ask him that would tell me if it was worth it for me to show up a third time.

We settled into our chairs and began talking. When the moment felt right, I looked him in the eye and asked, "How many gay people have you cured, and how many of them were women?"

Silence hung in the air as he fidgeted in his chair. He took a deep breath, avoided my gaze, and said, "I've worked with one young man."

"Did he change?" I asked.

Fritz looked down for a long time, then looked straight into my eyes and said, "No, he didn't."

Fritz had never turned a gay person into a straight one. All hope drained from my heart as his words sank in. He would not be able to help me because there was no help.

To satisfy the Bishop and my parents, I continued seeing Fritz for several weeks. It took me that long to come to terms with the real situation.

At the end of my last session, I told Fritz I didn't feel like therapy was helping me to change. He said, "If we could strip you naked and throw you into a swimming pool filled with naked lesbians, I think that would completely cure you."

I never went back.

Chapter 15
First Gay Friends

After I sped away from Fritz, I drove straight to my coach's office.

"Is there still a spot for me on the team?" I asked. The season had already started, and I figured I'd need to work hard to catch up.

With a huge smile, the coach said, "Absolutely, Marnie. Welcome to the team!"

I went home and told my parents I was finished with seeing Fritz. "He said there was nothing he could do for me," I said. "He did not have a plan for me, and he has never helped anyone change in the way we had hoped he could."

My parents were sad and disappointed, and to be truthful, so was I. I had placed a lot of faith in Fritz, and the people I most trusted believed he could change me.

Later, I told my parents I was going to play basketball. They were not pleased. They wanted me to keep my focus on church, school, and all efforts to change. Even though I was no longer seeing Fritz, I was still committed to going to church and seeing my bishop regularly. I decided I would just play basketball and not be gay.

Like the escapades I'd instigated with friends, basketball gave me temporary relief from my deep struggle. I played as hard as I could, and by the end of a three-hour practice, I was too exhausted to feel bad about myself. Games let me completely forget. I worked my way to the starting line-up and made a few friends. Off the court, I did homework, spent time with my family and friends, went to church, and prayed for a miracle.

There were two assistant coaches on the team. I suspected one was a lesbian. I had never knowingly encountered a gay woman before, so I was intrigued. I watched her closely even as I did everything to avoid her. I was not attracted to her in any way. Still, I didn't want to get too close to any lesbian in case I might fall over the edge. I was living a straight and focused life, going to school and playing basketball. I never acted on my feelings toward girls and didn't intend to.

One day before practice, I was in the gym shooting baskets. The assistant coach I had been avoiding came over to rebound balls for me. I could tell she had something on her mind.

"I'm a lesbian," she said.

I didn't act surprised, since I was pretty certain she was. There was something about the way she said it, though, that made me uncomfortable, as if she were baiting me. She studied me for a reaction.

If she was out to shock me, her next words did it. "Do you know that your friends on first string are all lesbians?" There were five of us on first string, including me.

I nearly choked. "No way!" I thought. I resented her telling me this. It felt inappropriate in every way. She was outing my friends while fishing to find out if I was gay, too. There was no way I would reward her with a response, much less an admission of something I was still fighting against being.

Instead, I went through the motions of practice that day feeling numb, only speaking when spoken to. My coach asked me if I felt okay, and I nodded. "Yeah," I said.

For a week, I went to practice, played ball, and went home. No hanging out, and no jokes or easy conversations like before. I couldn't eat or sleep and felt sick most of the time. I was doing all I could to stay away from anyone or anything gay, but it seemed to be all around me.

I decided I couldn't be friends with my teammates anymore. So, I played ball with them and left the rest behind.

Shortly after, the father of one of the girls on the team had a heart attack and died. I got the call early one morning that the team was going to Denise's house to be with her.

I went to Denise's house with the others. We spent three solid days grieving with her. What I saw was how the girls on my team came together for each other. Their empathy and compassion moved me. I realized these were some of the best friends I'd ever had, and I could not cut them out of my life. They were caring human beings, gay or not.

I stopped fighting the feelings. Instead, I just sort of sat with them.

At some point during those three days, I told my teammates that I was trying not to be gay and that it was hard for me that they were. They were incredibly supportive and understanding. For the first time, that part of me wasn't ugly and bad. What an incredible relief to feel their support and the absence of judgment.

A short time later, I informed my parents that I was not going to go to church anymore. We fought about it. I told them it was my decision because, at eighteen, I was an adult. Although this was true, honestly, I just couldn't handle the guilt any more. Every time I went to church, I felt like the worst person alive. They made it clear that if I was going to live in their house, I would have to follow their rules. After much disagreement, I agreed to their rules, and they accepted the fact that I was not going to go to church.

Gradually, things settled into the "new normal". I went to school, played basketball, and hung out with friends on the weekends. We played basketball, went out to eat, went to movies, or spent time at their apartments. It was different for me not to go to church, especially on Sunday mornings when my family was getting ready for church. But it also was a relief.

Chapter 16
My First Girl Kiss

Even though I was hanging out with gay friends, I was still not living what would be called a gay lifestyle. I had never gone to a gay event or even kissed a girl.

One night after a tournament, my friends told me they wanted to take me to a party and get me drunk. Mormons don't drink, and I had only tried alcohol once during high school. I agreed to party with everyone after the last game of the season.

When the big night eventually arrived, we drove over to the apartment where one of the players lived. We played a game called Mexicali, which I had never played before. We sat in a circle around a table. One person would bounce a quarter on the table and try to land it in a filled shot glass. If the quarter landed in the shot glass, the person who had tossed the quarter successfully would choose who would drink it, and kiss that person. As I sat waiting in that circle, I cannot even begin to explain the jumble of feelings that were coursing through my body.

I had not kissed a woman yet, nor had I ever seen two women kiss. First, Denise bounced the quarter on the table and it missed. Then Robyn bounced the quarter on the table and it missed again. I noticed I was holding my breath. When Michelle bounced the quarter next, it missed, and she looked relieved.

Then a girl with long brown hair, who I didn't know, bounced the quarter on the table, and it went in. She looked at me as she stood up. My first thought was to run. I was about to be kissed by a girl. Nervous tension pulsed through me like electricity.

She smiled as she walked slowly around the table to where I was sitting. Time stood still. She was beautiful. She bent down to me, looked directly into my eyes, and gave me several soft and gentle kisses.

Nothing could have prepared me for what I felt. I pulled back and tried to breathe. It was amazingly different than kissing boys. No comparison. It was like the difference between eating a yummy caramel covered in dark chocolate and eating one with a small sprinkle of sea salt on top. Both are good, but there is a delicious, delectable difference. Her kiss was delicious in a way I had never experienced before.

Chapter 17
My First Lesbian Dance

Like most college kids growing up in my area, hanging out with my friends around Pacific Grove and Monterey, California became a natural part of my life. I had never been to a women's dance, so when one was happening in Monterey, my friends insisted I join them.

I was only eighteen and was not certain they would let me in, so I tried to dress to look a little older. It makes me laugh now to recall the outfit I put together for the "big night." I wore white pants, a white shirt, a short red jacket and a little black bow tie.

I was very nervous on the drive over to the hall, so nervous, in fact, that as I got out of my car, I locked my keys inside. No way! What now? Luckily, two women pulled up at about the same time. One was a police officer, and to my great relief, she unlocked my door in no time.

I stayed outside the building for a moment to calm myself, and then carefully followed the instructions my friends had given me. I walked up to the door like it was no big deal, handed my money to the cashier, and stepped inside.

My friends had prepared me to get through the door, but nothing they shared with me would have prepared me for what I saw on the other side. It was amazing. The room was filled with women of all ages, all walks of life. They were not all jocks; many of them looked like the proverbial "woman next door." I felt as if I had stepped into a beautiful parallel universe. I stood there, taking it all in. Wow!

I felt conspicuous as I walked over to my friends, as though everyone was watching me. Maybe it was that red jacket or perhaps my awkwardness as a newbie. Either way, I was relieved to join the safe circle of my friends.

As silly as it might sound, the notion of actually getting out on the floor and dancing at this event hadn't even entered my mind. It took all I could muster to agree to show up, figure out what to wear, and get in the door underage. So I was surprised when I felt a tap on my shoulder. Slowly I turned to see who was tapping me.

She was tall, twice my age, with a crew cut and a gruff voice. "May I have this dance?"

Like a deer caught in headlights, I mumbled "Sure."

She put my arm in hers and escorted me to the dance floor. My partner for my first-ever dance with a woman was wearing a light blue tuxedo with a man's big black bow tie and a shirt with a blue-trimmed ruffle down the front, just like the boys wore to the prom. As we began to dance, my eyes went in the only direction they could bear - to the floor. I was horrified to see that she was wearing brown patent leather shoes that matched a pair my dad wore. Could it get worse?!

We danced three long songs before I thanked her and said I was tired. Later, when she tried to find me to dance again, my friends hid me from her. It was my first dance with a woman, but not quite the romantic moment I wanted.

As I started to feel a little more comfortable, I danced with a couple of different women and began to relax. Then I noticed a really beautiful woman with long, chestnut brown hair sitting at the bar. I walked to the opposite end of the bar and ordered a cranberry soda.

I was about to go over and sit down next to her when I saw a tall blonde walk up and ask her to dance. "No, thank you," she said. "I'm not into dancing."

Over the next fifteen minutes, I watched the same blonde return four times to ask the woman at the bar to dance. "Leave me alone," she said.

I have no idea how I got the courage, but I walked over and sat on the stool next to her.

"She certainly is persistent," I said.

The woman turned to me with a look of relief, and we began talking. She introduced herself as Diana Ramirez. I quickly realized she was at least ten to fifteen years older than me. Her big brown eyes looked sad to me.

"Are you okay," I asked.

"Honestly?" she said.

Our eyes met, and I said, "Yes, honestly."

Over the next thirty minutes, she tearfully told me about her terminally ill father who had just entered an extended care facility.

We were leaning toward one another so we could hear each other over the blaring music when I saw movement out of the corner of my eye. I was surprised to see the tall blonde hovering, still wanting to dance with Diana. What was she thinking?!

Diana was speechless. I took her by the hand and said to the blonde, "We were just on our way to dance." Diana looked at me gratefully.

As we walked onto the dance floor, a slow song was playing. With Morgan, at the Girls' Choice Dance the year before, slow dancing had been a chore. Not so now. It was my first dance with someone who was smaller than me, so I took the lead. I gently placed my arm around her back and took her hand. We danced with some distance between us for about a minute, then Diana pulled me close and said, "Thank you."

Her body felt incredible next to mine. We moved perfectly together and warmth spread through my entire body.

My basketball friends were riveted on us. It was hard not to smile. We danced a couple of songs, then Diana led me off the dance floor. Denise came over and introduced herself to Diana, mentioning that we were all going to a party in Pacific Grove, about fifteen minutes away. She invited Diana to join us. Diana looked at me. I nodded, and she said, "Okay." She said she needed to stop by her house on the way and that she and I would meet everyone at the party. I calmly said, "Sure."

I followed her to her house in my car. She stopped in front of a craftsman bungalow with a close cut lawn and flowers in the window boxes. She invited me in. I looked at the leather furniture, and matching end tables; this was not a college apartment. I wondered if she had any idea how young I was. She went into the bedroom for a minute, calling out for me to take off my jacket and relax.

"I'm fine," I said.

She emerged from her room and walked directly toward me. I stood there, not moving an inch, beginning to feel my palms sweat.

"Take off your jacket," she repeated.

"No, I'm fine," I answered again.

She came closer, then put her arms around my neck and began to kiss me playfully while sliding my jacket off my shoulders. I could smell a hint of perfume and cloves. The kisses went deeper and I pulled her tightly against me.

Immediately, my passion was interrupted by the message I had heard for years: "No sex before marriage." I pulled back, looking at Diana. She laughed and bit me softly on the lip. I could feel the heat from her beautiful body, and for a moment I told myself, "If I stay with her, nobody would ever really know."

But I couldn't do it. My Mormon morals ran too deep.

"I think we should go to the party to meet my friends," I said.

She laughed and said, "We will. Just sit down a minute."

Diana walked over to a glass coffee table and sat down on the couch. She opened a wooden box and I watched her spread two white lines of powder on the glass table.

I began stressing. Drugs had never been my thing. She took out what looked like a short glass tube and sniffed each line. In an instant, the evening was shattered for me.

"I have plenty to share," she said. "It's really great stuff."

"No thanks," I said.

"We could stay here, just the two of us," she said.

"No, I'd like to go meet up with my friends," I said. "We can hang out together over there."

Panic was setting in. I wanted to get out of there and away from this woman as quickly as possible. She slowly put on her jacket and we walked to our cars. I didn't offer to drive her.

Once inside my car, I let myself feel the shock of what had just happened. I didn't care how beautiful Diana was, I was not into that scene, and I couldn't wait to get back to the safety of my friends.

The party was being held at a huge and beautiful house. When we arrived, it was in full swing. People were dancing, making out, and going upstairs to bedrooms. Bottles of alcohol were everywhere.

Diana took me by the hand and led me into the middle of the pack of dancers. We danced hard until we were pouring sweat. Physical exercise always helped me to relax, and I actually started to have fun.

We started dancing closer. Diana took my hand and rolled her back into me, taking my other arm and wrapping it around her as well. She smelled intoxicating, and I felt that familiar warmth as she moved against me. Our bodies were completely in sync. The song ended, she turned and looked into my eyes and took me by the hand to lead me upstairs.

Instantly, I froze. I shook my head "No," let go of her hand, and left to go find a place to sleep. By then, it was three in the morning, and many of my friends were sleeping or passed out.

I found a small, narrow window bed and lay down to sleep, exhausted. I fell asleep for a couple of hours then woke with a start. It took me a minute to remember where I was, and then the guilt hit me, hard.

It was too early to go home, so I lay there another hour asking myself, "What the heck are you doing?!" The shock of what I had seen and experienced, the fact that I was there, plus the scrapes with sex and drugs, sent me running.

Chapter 18
Take Me Back

When basketball season ended, I didn't see my friends nearly as much. My studies had my attention, and a horrible sense of guilt nagged at me for having given in to acting like a lesbian around my gay friends, although I had not engaged in any activity beyond those initial kisses and dancing.

In my second quarter of school, my Psych 1A professor said there would be a class trip to a mental institution, originally known as the "great asylum for the insane" in Santa Clara County. The hospital was most famously known as the site of the greatest loss of life in Santa Clara County after the 1906 earthquake. Eleven officials and over 100 patients were crushed when the main treatment building had collapsed.

He explained the visit could be difficult emotionally, and for that reason, he would not permit students under twenty-one to go. I talked him into letting me go, even though I was only eighteen. After all, I thought, what could be so emotionally difficult about seeing people in a mental institution?

It was a beautiful California morning as we climbed into the van. Mary, a friend and teammate, was also in the class. She was about to transfer to Chico State and that became the topic of conversation on the hour-and-a-half drive to the facility.

As we pulled into the parking lot, the Mission style building reminded me of my old high school. My professor reviewed the rules for our visit and told us that we were there to experience and observe people in an institutional setting. We would not be visiting the floors holding violent patients or criminals.

The place smelled like a cross between an old folks' home and a hospital, like someone had mixed canned peas with disinfectant. A receptionist greeted us and repeated the rules once more. I could hear muffled sounds behind the closed doors nearby.

She pushed a button and the door to my left unlocked. We entered a long hallway with yellow-green walls and fluorescent lighting. The sound of our shoes echoed as we followed her to the first room.

She opened the door and we stepped into a day room filled with adults. Most were sitting, and many were talking to themselves, or crying or swaying. They were seemingly unaware that our group had entered. A few of them glanced at me as I walked by, but most maintained a hollow look in their eyes. I smiled nervously at them as we moved down the hallway, past small, sanitized dorm-like bedrooms, and then into another large space holding even more people.

I relaxed a little and said hello to those who made eye contact with me. This field trip was going to be manageable. Not emotionally difficult, just a little uncomfortable. But I had no idea what lay ahead.

My professor led us to the second floor, through double doors, and into a massive room containing rows of little kids lying on small mats or lying in cribs. We walked in a line, peering down at the children. They ranged in age from infants to ten-year olds. Some of their challenges were obvious, but many were not. The infants were swaddled in blankets and looked like any of the sweet little babies I'd ever seen.

A nurse joined us and explained that all of the babies had physical or mental disabilities and that many would not survive. I wondered who would love the babies while they were still alive? My feet felt heavy as we moved on.

The nurse stopped and called our attention to an adorable, curly-haired, blonde girl sitting on one of the mats. She appeared to be about four years old. She was born without a mouth or an esophagus and was fed through a tube. She had lived much longer than expected, although the nurse felt she could last only another year or two. Another year or two? To me, that seemed like forever.

Her bright blue eyes connected with mine. I smiled and waved at her. The line moved on.

I had taken about five steps when I felt something against my pant leg. The little girl had followed me. I bent down and she crawled into my arms. I held her close as I stood up, knowing I was breaking the rule about no physical contact. She touched my hair and face as I softly spoke to her. The nurse glanced at me several times. I smiled and looked away. She seemed torn about what to do.

I carried the little girl as we toured the rest of the room. When it was time to leave, I walked back to her mat and gently put her down. I told her she was a good little girl and that I needed to go now. She would have none of it. She tried to get back into my arms as my name was called from the door. I had to leave. I got up and walked away, holding back tears. I could hear her little footsteps running toward me, so I walked faster and slipped through the door, never looking back.

The experience had suddenly become emotionally unbearable. Numb, I toured the rest of the facility and made it to the van before crying. I didn't make a sound, but I could not stop my tears. Everyone in the van was silent as we drove home.

That night, as I held my four year-old sister and looked into her big brown eyes, I thought about the little girl at the institution. My sister had toys and pretty dresses and siblings fighting to hold her. She ran through the sprinklers, and enjoyed bedtime stories and kisses. She felt the green grass on her toes, and played under blue skies with big white fluffy clouds. The blue-eyed girl had none of this.

I was heartsick. I believed if the girl had been born into our family, or into any of the Mormon families I knew, she would have been kept and loved like my little sister.

I couldn't sleep. My thoughts turned to the love of my family and the safety of my church. My parents didn't try to get me to go against what I'd been taught. They didn't offer me alcohol, sex, or drugs. They didn't confuse me with choices that could destroy me. No, they wanted me safe and happy, and they had offered me a clear, though difficult, path to God. Yet, I had walked away.

Guilt swept over me as I thought of the love of my parents and the sacrifices they had made for me. I thought about one of my favorite childhood memories, which was a time when my brother and I were sitting on our wet towels out on our hot driveway at our house in Bountiful, Utah, We were eating peanut butter sandwiches as we listened to prop airplanes fly overhead.

I thought about the hundreds of basketball games my mom had watched me play. I thought about how she always made a special lunch for me on game days with my two favorite things, Cheetos and Martinelli's Apple Cider. I thought about the hours upon hours of board games my parents played with my brother and me, the family trips, dinners together every night, family home evenings, and family church meetings. I could count on it all. It was there, waiting for me.

Take Me Back

I wanted to go back. Life was too unpredictable out here, even dangerous. I craved the safety of my family, the guarantees of my church.

I would call the Bishop in the morning.

Chapter 19
BYU

I set up an appointment with Bishop Roberts. I confessed to him that I still felt the same way about women but wanted to change.

He said, "I think the answer for you is to go to BYU (Brigham Young University)." He added, "You just need to find the right boy, settle down, and get married. That will take care of this thing once and for all." How I prayed he was right.

I returned to my familiar Mormon lifestyle and hoped it would work. I went back to church, prayed, fasted, and read the scriptures. My parents were ecstatic. I applied to BYU and was accepted.

BYU students are asked to sign a behavioral "Code of Ethics." It was a lengthy document that made it clear what was expected of me. Rather than being turned off by it, I was happy for it. This was my best chance at being a normal Mormon girl, which I hoped with all of my being could be true.

My parents could not have been more proud. The girl they wanted me to be had returned to them. Maybe I would marry a good Mormon boy in the temple after all. Plus, I was the first grandchild to go to BYU, which sent a happy buzz throughout the extended family.

In the months before leaving for BYU, I stayed away from my basketball friends. I got a job at a mortuary helping people pick out gravestones for their family members, saved my money, went to church, and prepared to leave for school.

The day finally came for me to say goodbye to my brothers and sisters and leave with my parents for Salt Lake City, Utah. As nervous as I was, I couldn't wait. We stayed a night with my grandparents, and my aunts and uncles came to congratulate me. My mom and dad were so proud of me. I felt genuinely happy.

The next morning, we left for Provo, Utah, home of the BYU Cougars. I could not believe how huge the campus was and wondered how I'd ever find my way around. As soon as we arrived, we got a phone call - Grandmother Josephine had just had a stroke. My parents promised they would return to her as soon as they got me to my room.

We carried my things to the dorm elevator. I pushed the button for the sixth floor and we made our way to Room 618 of Deseret Towers. My roommate had already moved in, so we began to unload my things in the empty half of the space.

I kissed my parents goodbye, assured them I would be fine, and then had the urge to run after them like an eight-year old. I felt scared and alone. I closed the door and sat on my bed. My eyes went to my roommate's side of my new home-away-from-home. I could not believe what I saw. Her walls were covered with pictures of President Kimball, the same man who was the former prophet of the Mormon Church and the author of *The Miracle of Forgiveness,* pictures of Jesus, and a bunch of crafty homemaking stuff.

Based on what I saw, I knew my roommate and I could not be more different. Our college applications had asked for our interests. I assumed they would pair me with someone like myself who loved sports, hiking, and the outdoors. I was so wrong.

The door opened, and in walked Molly Mormon, homemaker. She shook my hand and introduced herself as Katrina. My next thought was: How am I going to live with this person for an entire year?

Luckily, Claire from upstate New York lived in the room next to us. She was the type of person I thought I would have been matched with as a roommate. We loved the same things; we played sports, loved to laugh, and stayed up late at night. We took school seriously, but having fun was a priority.

Claire and her roommate weren't a match either. Our roommates started hanging out with each other, which took some pressure off of us to spend time with them.

School was a blast. Days were spent in class and nights were spent studying and having fun. We ate pizza, watched movies, played intramural sports, cheered at BYU football games, danced until our feet ached, and hung out at the Wilkinson Student Center. I was living in full optimism that the worst of my life was behind me and that the future would unfold perfectly for me as promised by that long ago speaker from when I was twelve years old in my mutual class. He had promised that if we kept the commandments and attended early morning seminary, one day we would be married in the temple.

Chapter 20
James

One day, a friend and I walked over to the Union center for ice cream. A friend of my friend then introduced us to his cousin, James. James was tall and handsome. He had big blue eyes, light brown hair, and a moustache. I noticed he was watching me with interest as we talked. I was glad because I was watching him, too.

I was committed to being straight, and James seemed like the kind of guy I could enjoy being with, like John had been. I told my friend I wanted to get to know James, and we came up with a group date idea. The plan was to invite five couples to go out together. My job was to find a creative way to ask James to be my date.

James would be the first guy I dated since the time I had hung out with my lesbian friends.

I recalled having invited Morgan to the Girls' Choice Dance with a poem, so I decided to do the same for James. This one came with clues to solve instead of candy bars. If his answer to my invitation was *yes,* he was to stand outside my dorm window and sing a funny song at a specific time. I figured this was a good way to find out if he was my kind of guy or not.

At the designated time, I heard someone singing. I slid open my window, and there was James, six stories below, singing as loudly as he could on the lawn. He won me over.

We had a great time on our date, bowling with all of our friends, sharing a hot fudge sundae, and talking late into the night. James was a gentleman, and when he walked me to my dorm room, he asked me if I would like to go out again, and sweetly said goodnight. We began dating, and we seemed to be a good match. He was understanding about my need to have plenty of time with my other friends, and things were going really well.

One night, James and I decided to go out for a walk. He pulled me close and kissed me. I was okay with it. When Claire found out we had kissed, she went wild, jumping back and forth between our beds. I laughed.

Another day, James invited me to walk with him to the grocery store. James was easy for me to talk to, so when we got to the store I told him I needed to buy some tampons. This would be the first time I would buy tampons on my own. My mom had always done it.

We wandered around the store, looking for the tampons. James said, "Let's ask somebody."

"I'm too embarrassed to ask," I said. "I'll just buy them another time."

James insisted. He walked right up to the grocery checker, who was serving a long line of students. "Excuse me, where would I find the tampons?" It was yet another moment that proved to me I was dating a great guy.

James was easy to be with. He was a convert to the Mormon Church and seemed less rigid than the Mormon guys I had dated in the past. He never seemed judgmental of others, which let me relax into a gentle flow with him without pressure to be someone I wasn't.

Chapter 21
Roommates and Rumbles

I loved college. The constant dread I had carried for years appeared to be on hiatus. I studied hard and played hard, this time not to escape dread but to enjoy life. I earned top grades, was a teacher in my college Ward, and lived a straight Mormon life. I was happy.

Claire liked playing pranks and having spontaneous fun as much as I did. The first week of school, I was sitting on the lawn with a bunch of the gals from our dorm floor. Claire brought out her boom box and played it quietly. People walking by joined our little group, so we turned up the volume and started dancing. We were having a really great time, and then about thirty minutes into it, someone took ahold of my arm.

Claire and I were escorted to Standards, she, for owning the boom box, and me, for instigating the dance. How'd they know? We were told we hadn't gone through the required channels to have a dance, plus the hems of our shorts were just above our knees, a violation of the dress code.

When we got back to the dorm, everybody was waiting for us. As we walked down the hallway, they asked us what happened. "Not much," we said. "We just got a warning."

It wasn't the last time I went to Standards for spontaneous dances near the student center, but the fun was always worth it.

On another night, Claire and I offered a nearly-impossible challenge to our friends: "Let's see if we can climb over the pool fence at midnight, skinny dip across the pool, put our clothes back on, and climb back over the fence again without getting caught."

Several girls took us up on the challenge.

The dorms were high-rise buildings that surrounded the pool. Half of them were for girls and half were for boys. At midnight our group gathered and snuck out of our dorm. We put a shoe in the door to get back in.

There were no lights on in or around the pool, so our challenge would be completed in darkness. We climbed the high metal fence in silence.

Once over the fence, all but one of us dropped our clothes and slipped into the water, then raced across to the other side. I never realized swimming was so noisy, even when you are trying to be quiet.

All was going as planned, until Claire swam into the wall and split open her lip. There in the dark, we started laughing. Suddenly, a light went on just outside the fence. And just as suddenly, girls were jumping out of the water pulling dry clothes onto their wet bodies, dropping pieces of clothing along the way. We ran back to the fence, climbed over, and ran for our dorm.

Unbelievably, we were not caught, but the clothing we left behind ended up in lost and found, never to be reclaimed.

A couple of weeks later, Claire and some girls ran to find me. "Something is wrong with Katrina," they said. Even though I could hardly tolerate her, I certainly didn't wish her any harm. We ran back to our room and found Katrina sobbing and thrashing uncontrollably in her bed. People around her were trying to comfort her, but it wasn't working.

I did what seemed right in the moment. I knelt down by her bed, placed my hands on her head, and began praying. The others knelt with me, touching her lightly as well. Usually only Mormon men lay their hands on someone's head in prayer. I can't remember what I said, but I believed in my heart I was doing the right thing. When my prayer was finished, we continued to quietly kneel around her, still comforting her. Eventually she fell asleep.

I never knew what caused Katrina to break down like that, but it was reason enough for Claire and I to agree we needed to swap roommates. We were great friends, and so were Katrina and Karen. Our housemother, Sister White, gave her approval and our roommates agreed. After all, Claire and I both liked sports, we were both messy, and we both liked to sleep with the window open, which was a constant bone of contention. Katrina didn't want to catch a chill.

After that, our room became the place to hang out. People looked to us for fun, and we delivered.

One night about ten girls were visiting us, and we decided to go bowling at the Wilkinson Center. On the way, I suggested we take a shortcut across a small canal. I was the first to go. I got a running start and jumped over to the other side. Claire followed, getting only one foot wet. The next eight people jumped but fell back into the canal, getting soaked. It was hilarious. We laughed until we cried and I thought I'd wet my pants. We never made it to bowling and somehow no one got sent to Standards.

Not all of our pranks ended with such good luck. There was the night four of us got together and filled all the trashcans in the building with water and leaned them against every door on the seventh floor. Once the cans were in place, we ran down the hall knocking on all the doors, hearing girls scream as gallons of water poured across their feet and into their rooms. We were shocked by the amount of water a trashcan could hold.

The dorm went into lockdown until the culprits came forward. My conscience got the better of me and I confessed to Mrs. White, knowing there would be consequences and a hefty bill for damages.

"You couldn't have done this alone," she said. "Who did it with you?"

I wasn't going to squeal on my friends, so I said, "I'll talk to them and let them decide to turn themselves in." They did. We each had to pay $250 for carpet cleaning. Mercifully, in spite of her being upset with us, Sister White let us pay it off in small amounts each month so our parents would never know. She also didn't send us to Standards. Months later, I learned from my parents that Sister White really liked me. Thank goodness. I've often wondered if she was the one who turned the light on at the pool and had let it go at that.

Things were still going well with James. One beautiful day, we decided to hike to the top of the mountain that has the "Y" on it for BYU. It was a difficult hike and few ever completed it. The top fourth of the mountain consisted of rock facings, going straight up. Some of the drops were high enough that James, who was 6'4", would put me up on his shoulders. Then I would step into his hands and he would stretch his arms as high as he could so I could stand up and reach the next precipice with the tips of my fingers and pull myself up. Then I would reach down and help pull him up to where I was.

After many hours of climbing, we reached the top. The view of the Provo Valley was breathtaking. There was one small, lone tree at the top the mountain. Hanging on the tree was a canister. Together we walked over and opened it, wondering what we'd find inside. It housed a journal of wishes that had been written by BYU students who had climbed the mountain. Some of the entries were decades old, dated and signed. Many of the wishes named a person they hoped to marry.

James said, "Shall we write our wishes?"

"Yes, but secretly," I answered.

I don't know what James wrote, but I wrote that I wished to fall in love with James and marry him one day. More than anything, I hoped this would be possible. We secured the lid on the canister and returned it to the limb of the wishing tree. Before we left the mountaintop, James took me in his arms and kissed me. We were becoming more passionate with one another, and he was a great kisser.

I was sure with time I would start to feel the "wow."

At BYU, I convinced myself that I was having the best time of my life. And for the most part, without the guilt of being a lesbian hanging over my head, it was.

I was excited to go home for Christmas. My family's Christmases together were wonderful, and I missed my parents and sisters and brothers. I brought along a BYU friend from Durban, South Africa, and was happy that she would be able to share in our Christmas. Since my youngest sister was only four-years old, we would even have a visit from Santa.

The entire family was waiting up for us when we arrived late that night. Everything was going as planned, and anyone looking in would never have known that, just a year before, I had been a horrible disappointment to my family.

Our family tradition on Christmas Eve was to prepare delicious appetizers, play games, and listen to my dad read *The Night Before Christmas.* Then everyone would open one present.

Christmas Eve was absolutely my favorite evening of the year. I loved it.

I was helping clear the table to get ready for games when Mom said "Bishop Roberts and his family will be spending Christmas day with us. We have become good friends since you've been away."

I couldn't believe my ears. That old familiar knot returned, along with the shame I felt from my talks with the Bishop. Even though I had gone back to him for help, and enrolled at BYU at his suggestion, the thought of sharing Christmas with Bishop Roberts made me sick.

When he and his family arrived at the door, I smiled politely and shook his hand. He avoided my eyes and said, "Welcome home, Marnie."

Being with the Bishop took me back to that feeling of being judged by him as someone between a murderer and a pedophile. Even though my parents did not know he had said that to me, it felt like a betrayal to have him in our home, especially on Christmas Day.

Chapter 22
Samantha

We returned to BYU after Christmas break. I was the Spiritual Living Teacher in my student ward. I loved to teach and put a lot of time and effort into preparing my lessons.

On my first Sunday back at the campus, I was halfway through my lesson when the most stunning woman I had ever seen walked into the room and took a seat near the front. I caught my breath and just stood there, looking at her, mesmerized. With great effort, I recalled the point where I had trailed off and pulled myself back to my lesson. As I resumed speaking, I kept glancing her way. It was hard for me to keep my eyes off of her. I finished my lesson, gathered my books, and went to introduce myself. Her name was Samantha Turner, "Sam" to her friends. She was from Huntington Beach, California. We immediately hit it off.

Every Sunday I met James for lunch. On this day, I did my best to stay focused on him, but my eyes searched for Sam. Eventually, I saw her come in and sit at a table across the room. When James and I put our trays away after lunch, I purposely walked by her. She noticed me.

Sam's room was directly below mine. It was a new term, and I was excited to discover that we shared two classes in common. We began walking to and from class and occasionally ate lunch together. I continued dating James but didn't feel the same excitement about seeing him that I did whenever I saw Sam. Her energy was like a magnet to me. The more I resisted, the harder it pulled.

Sam was often surrounded by guys who seemed captivated by her, too. Her golden brown hair, big brown eyes, and amazing smile were irresistible. She was undoubtedly among the most beautiful women they had ever seen. I understood how they felt. For me it wasn't just her physical beauty; there was something else about her.

Sam and I spent more and more time together and a lot less time with guys. We met innocently in friendship, but something was starting to happen inside of me that hadn't happened with anyone else, ever. We ate meals together, talked late into the night, and studied.

Meanwhile, I ignored a mounting worry.

Still, I made time for fun with my roommate, Claire. One weekend, I invited Claire and six girls from our dorm to my Gram's house for an overnighter and homemade food. We were trying to figure out how we were going to get to Salt Lake City, a little over an hour away, and somebody suggested we try Rent-A-Wreck. Claire and I headed there immediately.

First the guy showed us his "nice" models. Let's just say his definition and my definition of "nice" were very different. Regardless, we couldn't afford any of them.

"So how much money do you have," he asked.

"Forty dollars," we said.

He took us around the back of the building to an incredibly ugly car with four flat tires. He said it hadn't been driven in a while, but he could have the tires pumped up in no time.

Twenty minutes later, Claire and I were on our way back to the dorm to pick up the rest of the girls. We ran upstairs and told everyone we had a car, omitting the part about how they might feel riding in it. As we drove through campus, Claire ducked her head as the other girls laughed with embarrassment.

We spent an incredible night with my Grams. She fed us all the BBQ chicken we could eat, and we laughed until midnight. The following morning we went down to our car to find all four tires flat. Grams laughed hysterically. I loved her laugh.

From the time that I was a little girl, I knew my grandmother Lucy loved me with all her heart. I have many fond memories of us playing "Old Maid" for hours, sleeping out in her back yard, cuddling up in her bed after my Uncle Brad told us stories of Big Foot, and listening to her famous story of "Squeaky the Mouse and the Chocolate Cake." Grams had 27 grand kids, and to this day, each of us can still recite this story perfectly.

My friends from BYU loved my Grams too. Several times a month, she drove to Provo from Salt Lake City for movies, bowling, football games, and even to sleep in the dorm with us. We played games and laughed late into the night. I was so lucky to live close enough to spend time with her. Until I went to BYU, we had always lived a considerable distance apart.

One night, Sam and I went out with some girlfriends to dance at a disco owned by the Osmond family. It was late when we got back, so everyone went directly to their rooms. I walked Sam back to her room. Her roommate was already in bed, asleep.

Lately, we had begun giving each other a lot of neck and shoulder rubs, and it was my turn to give her a back rub. I started rubbing her shoulders and massaging her head. I could feel the energy growing between us. I could tell by the way she was moving that she was feeling the same. Eventually, she lay down on the bed, took my hand, and pulled me down beside her. I lost myself in her eyes. I had never experienced anything like it.

Slowly, Sam came toward me and our lips touched for the very first time. A charge of energy moved throughout my body. I closed my eyes and took a breath to breathe her in. Our lips parted and we began to explore, slowly, softly and gently.

Sam's roommate was sleeping in her bed right next to us. I nervously looked over at her, but she didn't seem to stir. Sam started to guide my hands, and gently I ran my fingers along her arms, and then along her back, and then onto her stomach.

More than anything in the world, I wanted her. But I couldn't do it. I couldn't get past all the voices in my head telling me it was wrong. We both agreed to stop.

For a long time we held one another. It was incredible, it was beautiful, and it was everything I had ever hoped to feel toward another human being. At the same time, it was torturous and excruciatingly painful because I believed I was going to be cast into outer darkness, the Mormon description of hell.

Eventually, I left Sam and went up to my room. Claire was asleep, and I slipped into bed without a sound. The next morning Sam and I met as usual for breakfast, and then we walked to class together. We didn't mention what had happened the night before, but our new closeness was palpable.

After class, we walked back to the dorm for lunch, stopping by Sam's room first to drop off her books. We found a note on her door instructing Sam to see Sister White immediately. Sam slowly opened her door, and we saw that her roommate had moved out. We stood there looking at one another as the reality sunk in. We were dead. How could we have been stupid enough to believe her roommate was sleeping?!

We ran up to my room to find a note on my door that told me to go to the Head of Standards. I was terrified. I hugged Sam, who looked scared to death, and I told her it would be okay. We were both shaking. I left her as she went to Sister White's apartment, and I started my walk to Standards.

By the time I got there, I had imagined every possible response. What was he going to say to me? I had been to Standards many times before, but never to meet with the Head of Standards, Richard Stewart.

"I'm Marnie Freeman," I said to his secretary. She directed me to a chair, and I waited in complete terror.

The Head of Standards ushered me to his office and into a hard seat. I was more than willing to face the consequences, but I could tell by the look of disdain on his face that it was going to be bad.

"Tell me what happened," he said. I told him the whole story.

"Are you telling me the truth," he asked.

"Absolutely," I said. I had no reason to lie. I believed in taking responsibility for what I did.

"Samantha's roommate says it didn't quite go that way," he said. "She says that you forced Samantha to participate, speaking harshly to her, and that Samantha answered you in a meek, timid voice and did everything you asked."

Luckily for me, Sam set the record straight. We were equally responsible for what had happened the night before.

Sam and I met back in her room. She looked as rough as I felt. I put my arms around her, and she laid her head on my shoulder. There was so much to talk about, but neither of us spoke. Instead, we quietly embraced in the eye of the storm, breathing in our closeness and pushing out thoughts of BYU, Standards, parents, and church. For a moment, we were safe from all of it.

We stepped back from one another, still holding hands tightly.

Once again, I was sick to my stomach with a choking lump in my throat. We reviewed each of our meetings with Standards. She was treated very differently than me, because Mr. Stewart still felt I was at fault and that Sam was an innocent victim.

"Thank you for telling the truth about last night," I said.

She looked into my eyes, and said, "I would never make you take the blame for something we both did."

"They will probably call our parents," I said. "Your mother is going to hate me."

"There is no way she will hate you," Sam said. "She just has to meet you and see who you are. There is no way she couldn't like you." I hoped she was right, but doubted it.

I met with the Head of Standards several times, as well as my BYU Bishop. My parents were called and asked to come to the campus. Surprisingly, they were kind and loving to me, in spite of the circumstances. I am sure they could tell how badly I felt and that I, again, was willing to do anything to change. Mom brought me a new Easter dress and shoes, sweetly wrapped with a bow. I appreciated her effort to bring some normalcy to our lives.

Sam's parents came to campus also; however, we never met. Once they arrived, the plan from Standards began immediately.

Sam and I were told to never see one another again, which was difficult since we lived in the same dorm, had classes together, and ate in the cafeteria. Still, we agreed.

Beyond that, Sam and I were treated differently. The Head of Standards learned that I had felt these feelings previously, so the plan for me was to see a private therapist in Provo who had agreed to work with me. First, he met with my parents, then invited me into their meeting. He told me his calendar was full for the next three weeks and that I would meet during that time with a therapist on campus.

In addition, I was ordered to go to Standards to sit in front of Mr. Stewart for thirty minutes every afternoon at 2:30. Each day, he stared at me with disgust. It was the most humiliating thing I have ever had to endure. To me, his absence of compassion seemed to be an evil greater than any sin Sam and I had committed.

My feelings for Sam were the strongest force I had ever felt in my life, stronger than the dread that I was a lesbian, and certainly stronger than anything I had ever felt for a guy. If I had ever felt anything for a guy like I felt for Sam, I would have absolutely married him.

The day came for my first therapy appointment with the campus counselor. I felt a bit edgy as I walked to his office, and, of course, I was skeptical. My expectations were low. I'd been down this road before, and the promises didn't pan out, plus this guy was a temp. The real pro was the therapist in Provo.

After a short wait in his outer office, he invited me in. I sensed that he was a kind person who had no intention of humiliating me. I spent the next hour-and-a-half relating what had happened that night with Sam, including all I had done before I had come to BYU. I figured in order for him to help me, he needed to know the entire truth. He needed to know that this was something I had felt for as long as I could remember.

When I finished, he studied me for a long time, his hand under his chin.

"I know the answer," he said.

"You do?" I asked. I was shocked and curious to hear what he had to say. Could he actually offer a solution?

He looked directly into my eyes and said, "You are afraid of penises. All you need to do is read this book, and I think it will take care of everything." He handed me the book.

This time, I did not fall for it. I knew he was wrong. No book was going to change something so deep inside of me. To be agreeable, I said I'd read it. I glanced through the book as I walked back to my dorm.

The first picture, of course, was of a penis. I honestly didn't have a response one way or the other to it. The issue had never been about me not enjoying being physical with someone who had a penis. I loved John and was growing to love James. True, I was low on penis experience, but they didn't scare me.

What scared me was that I might never hold Sam again. I did everything I could to stay away from her. But each night I could hear her come into her room, one floor below me. She no longer had a roommate, so all the sounds of movement were hers. Out the window, I could see when she turned her light on and when she turned it off. I could hear when she got up in the morning and knew when she slipped into her sheets at night. I knew she slept on her left side, with her hands tucked under her chin, and I tortured myself recalling the sound of her breath and the look of her eyelashes on her cheeks as she slept. I knew her gasps of pleasure when I ran my fingers along her hip and the scent of her skin. I couldn't get her out of my mind any more than I could get the sun out of the sky. She was there, warming me even when I tried to force her out of my mind.

My roommate, Claire, knew something was wrong, but she had no idea about what it was. My main focus was to keep my torn-apart self together so no one would suspect. The fun Claire and I had enjoyed gradually faded away. I continued to go to Standards every day, feeling like a kindergartner sitting with my nose in the corner, except my nose was four feet away from the nose of Mr. Richard Stewart, Head of BYU Standards.

Chapter 23
Please Leave

Late one night, I wanted to take a good long run to relieve my stress and sadness. As I stepped off the elevator to go outside, I saw Sam sitting on a couch with six guys around her. I caught her eye and could see she was enduring the same torture as me.

I ran as fast and as hard as I possibly could. Running took the edge off the pain, and I had been doing a lot of it. It was snowing, but I ran anyway. I headed toward the hills and could see the temple shining in the distance. Without realizing it, I ran toward the temple at top speed, snowflakes stinging my eyes. I felt like I was running for my life, and no matter how fast I ran I could not outrun the torture I felt inside.

As I came to the front of the temple I fell to my knees. I cried bitter tears as I screamed at God. There in front of His temple, I screamed that He had forsaken me, that I had done all the things I was supposed to do, and still He had forsaken me. I stayed there on my knees, sobbing, asking God why He had not made me normal.

Eventually, I stopped crying. I looked up at the temple, and for the first time I knew there were no answers for me, regardless of what anyone said, guaranteed, or hoped for. I was stuck with this "thing," I was not normal, and there was nothing that could be done to change it.

Slowly, I got to my feet and walked back to the dorm. Sam was still on the couch. I hoped she could not see my pain.

I took the elevator to the sixth floor, and just as I put my key in the door, I heard her call my name. I turned and she came to me.

In tears, she said, "I can't do this anymore. I miss you. I can't stand not being with you. I hate acting like we don't know each other." And then she was in my arms.

She took me by the hand, and we walked down to her room. No one was in the hall. Our gentle kisses turned passionate. I couldn't get enough of her, nor she of me. She had been ripped out of my life, and I could not stand another minute without her.

Slowly, we lay down on the bed, and she pulled me on top of her. I purposely slowed down to feel every minute. She slid my hand inside her shirt. I traced her rib cage, feeling the softness of the edge of her breast, resisting my desire to touch her. With all of my being, I wanted her.

My mouth found hers again and she met me passionately, pulling me tightly against her. I knew I was just getting started, and if I had any hope of not making love to her completely, I had to end it now. I looked at her and said, "We'd better stop or I won't be able to."

Somehow, we both agreed. I slid onto my side and pulled her in next to me. I spooned my body around hers, and she snuggled in. Our clothes were still on and we had not gone to that place of no return.

Sam softly traced the palm of my hand with her fingers. I butterfly-kissed the back of her neck. I loved this woman. Nothing had ever felt so completely right.

I woke the next morning and lay there watching her, knowing it would be the last time I would ever be with her like this. I listened to her soft breathing and studied her innocent face. She was so beautiful.

When she woke up, I said, "We've got to tell the Bishop." She didn't try to talk me out of it. I knew it would probably mean

I'd be sent home.

At 7:30 AM, I called the Bishop and told him what had happened. The Bishop sadly told me he had no recourse but to notify Standards. I told him I understood.

By 8:00 AM, I was at the Standards Office and officially expelled from Brigham Young University. I asked about credit for my classes. We were near the end of the term and my grades were good. I didn't want to lose them. The Head of Standards said he would take care of it, that I would receive official withdrawals from my classes, not failures.

As I turned to leave, Richard Stewart, head of BYU Standards, said, "If it were up to me you would never step foot on this campus, you would never step foot in Provo, and you would never be allowed back in to this state. We do not need people like you."

His words hurt, but were nothing compared to the pain I already felt - the pain that I was who I was, the pain that I would never see Sam again, and the pain that I would soon face my parents and all the people in my church back in California.

The daughter of the recently-named President Freeman was being sent home from Brigham Young University.

I called James and told him we needed to talk. We sat on a brick wall facing one another. He knew something was wrong. Finally, I told him I was being sent home, but I didn't tell him why. I couldn't. He was very sweet. He took my face in his hands, looked into my eyes, and said there wasn't anything we couldn't work through together. I looked at him, kissed him softly on the cheek, and said, "No, we can't work through this."

I looked at James one last time and walked away.

Sam came to my room as I was packing. She had been given the choice to stay at BYU or go home, and she chose to go home. She didn't feel it was fair for her to stay if I had to go home.

She had gone to the campus bookstore and bought me a gift. It was an oval, cream-colored plaque with a black etching of a Mormon woman on her knees, in prayer. I was confused by what it meant, but didn't ask. We held each other in a long embrace, then we parted, with plans to stay in touch.

By 10:00 AM, I was completely packed and waiting downstairs for my Aunt Mary Ann to pick me up to take me to Salt Lake City to catch a bus for home. I sat on my boxes as my friends walked by. They seemed puzzled but didn't talk to me. I felt alone and ashamed.

As I waited for what seemed forever for my aunt to arrive, a familiar voice called my name. I turned to see an old childhood friend from California, John's sister. A few years older than me, she was also a student at the Y. When my family first arrived in California, years before, she had taken me under her wing. I don't know how she heard I was being sent home, and I never asked, but she hugged me goodbye and gave me a bag of Cinnamon Bears, which had become one of my favorite candies since the days when my dad would give them to my brother and me as a treat for helping him work on Saturdays.

It was surreal to sit there on my boxes staring at the bag of Cinnamon Bears, waiting for my ride away from BYU, Sam, my friends, the classes, my teaching, and the fun.

I spotted Mary Ann's van as it turned into the parking lot. She was someone I felt close to. Part of me couldn't wait to find comfort in her; the other part of me wanted to turn and run back to my room, wishing this were all a bad dream. After my boxes were loaded into her car, I turned and looked at Deseret Towers one last time, then climbed into my seat.

"Are you okay?" she asked.

"Yes, fine," I said.

We drove in silence all the way to Salt Lake City. I could tell she wanted to talk to me, comfort me, but did not know what to say. Mary Ann is my mother's youngest sister and had always been my favorite aunt. Through everything that had gone on in years past, she did not seem to judge me or be disappointed in me. There in the car, in the thick silence, I could tell she still loved me just as much as before. It felt to me like she was sad about my pain, not about who I was or the choices I had made.

Words cannot express how badly I felt. I lost everything.

James was the only friend I was able to say goodbye to that morning. I called Claire a few months later, but she wouldn't come to the phone. We never spoke again.

Mary Ann pulled into the Greyhound bus station where my ticket was waiting for me. Only four hours had passed since I had left Sam's arms and called the Bishop. My exit was swift and well-orchestrated.

Mary Ann hugged me goodbye. As she turned to leave, I could see the tears in her eyes.

I checked all of my boxes. The only thing I carried onto the bus was my bag of Cinnamon Bears. I never opened the package; I just held onto it. They were a symbol of kindness from a friend, and I didn't want to let go.

It took about twenty hours to travel to my one and only layover, San Francisco. I stood in the fenced area and looked out over the city, a city I had heard held a big population of gay people. I was tempted to climb over the fence and run away, deep into the city. I knew there were people like me there, but I had no idea where to find them. I was crushed by a loneliness I'd never known.

Finally, the number for my bus was announced and I got in line. When I looked down to hand the bus driver my ticket, I was still holding my bag of Cinnamon Bears.

I got on the bus, found a seat next to a window, and sat down. As the bus pulled out of the station, I had two thoughts: This was my last chance to run away, and I was only two-and-a-half hours away from Salinas where I would have to face my family, my friends, and my church. I was heartsick.

The last leg of my bus ride went very quickly, but there was still plenty of time for fear to mount. I was so scared. I was the last to get off the bus, and to my surprise no one was there to meet me. This was the first and only time in my life that someone was not waiting to meet me when I came home. My heart froze, and I knew things would never be the same.

I waited about half-an-hour until Mom finally arrived. There was no hug. She asked me quietly to get my things. My mom didn't seem to know what to do with me. I didn't know what to do with me, either.

I loaded my boxes into the car and we drove home in a nightmarish silence that made it way too easy to hear the cries from inside, begging for someone to tell me I was loved, that I was okay.

Chapter 24
I Try Life as a Lesbian

I didn't know it at the time, but my parents had told my brother and two sisters why I'd left BYU. They cried and comforted each other. My two younger siblings were not told, although my little brother later recalled sensing something terrible had happened. I didn't know they knew, but their silence made the walls of isolation feel even thicker.

When my dad got home from work, my parents told me they wanted to speak with me. I wondered if they were going to ask me to leave. They listed the rules I would live by if I stayed in their house. They said I could move back into my old room with my sister Carri, and told me they had found a therapist who would work with me. They said they did not have any understanding of this whole thing and that it was a shame I had given up so much.

I sat there, taking it in, not daring to say a word.

For the first three days, I only came downstairs for meals and spent the rest of the time in my room. I walked the streets at night when everyone was asleep. I felt lost, with no idea as to what to do. Sometimes I prayed, sometimes I cried, but mostly I just walked.

Then Sunday came, the day of absolute terror. Saturday night was sleepless and Sunday morning was sickening. I had to go to church and face all the people I had grown up with, the people who had loved me, taught me, and encouraged me, the people whose kids I had played with and even led. Their kids were still at university, and I had been sent home.

The ride to church with the whole family was the quietest I ever remember. I fought back the tears as we pulled into the parking lot, stepped out of the car, and walked through the doors.

Instead of their usual hugs and laughter when they saw me, Sister Lowe and Brother Hendricks, two of my favorite people and the parents of my close friends, did not speak to me. Neither did Sister Layton, a big fan of mine who once told me she would be proud to have one of her sons marry me, leaning in to say she wouldn't say that to many girls.

When I realized no one was going to talk to me, I found my way to the chapel and sat down. My little sister, Carri, came in and sat by me, opening the songbook for us to hold together. I felt her gentle kindness. During the opening song, tears streamed down my face and Carri began crying, too. Without looking at me, she slid closer, the first act of affection anyone had shown me since I got home. It meant so much to me that someone in my family still loved me.

I had thought people weren't talking to me because I had been expelled from BYU; however, years later I learned that Bishop Roberts had broken the code of confidentiality, telling people why I had been sent home.

I went to church another three weeks, until I could no longer handle the silence, the looks, and the unspoken judgment. I still wanted to be Mormon, but until I could figure out a way to be normal, it would be hard for people to be with me like before. My parents were heartbroken.

Even though Sam and I had both returned home, we were still under the "No Contact" rule. Secretly, we spoke on the phone, and I sent letters to a friend's address she had given me. Sometimes we talked, sometimes we cried, but neither of us had any idea as to what to do. One night, Sam seemed particularly upset. After a while, she said, "I am sad, I am confused, and my parents and Bishop don't want me to have anything to do with you. I feel like I need time to figure things out."

Her words crushed me, but I understood. I had one request. "Regardless of what your decision is," I said, "please call and tell me yourself." She promised she would.

Sam didn't keep her promise, and I never heard from her again. I swallowed my sadness and closed the door on her. I told myself if she didn't keep her promise, she must not have really cared about me.

From the time I was sent home, I had regular therapy sessions with Dr. Rhonda Harlow. She was not Mormon, and I thought that was a huge plus. She came highly recommended to my parents or I'm sure they never would have let me see her. About six weeks into therapy, Dr. Harlow looked at me and said, "Marnie, you need to accept who you are."

"What? I can't just accept this about myself," I said.

Again she said, "Marnie, you need to come to terms with who you are."

Her words put me into a complete panic. "I am seeing you so I can change. How can you tell me to just accept who I am?"

"Some people are born gay," she said. "I think you are one of them."

Her words shocked me. Was it possible I came into this world already gay? That being gay was a part of me just like my dark hair and eyes? Was it possible I had not done something wrong to cause this to happen, to make God so mad at me that he wouldn't help me be like everyone else?

Dr. Harlow said it was possible that, for me, being gay was normal. If I was born gay, then gay was my normal. Not being gay would not be normal for me.

As evil as the idea seemed, a sense of relief washed over me as I let the notion sink in. It would be such an incredible relief to stop fighting who I was. I toyed with the comforting thought that possibly my love for Sam was a normal response for a woman born gay.

These thoughts intrigued, yet frightened, me. I wanted them to be true, but according to what I had been taught, they were lies.

I hardly slept, walking the streets past homes with families that fit the formula. I didn't fit and because of that my whole family didn't fit. In the Mormon Church, if everyone in the family lives a life of worthiness, they will be together in the Celestial Kingdom. If I stayed on this path, I would no longer be a part of my family in that sense. They would be in. I would be out.

My parents were desperately trying to rein me back in and keep our celestial family together, not just on this earth but forever.

After several more weeks of therapy, I decided to make the leap into life as a lesbian, whatever that meant. I would try out my "normal."

One of my coaches from Hartnell College invited me on a backpacking trip with five other women, all of whom were couples. We drove over fourteen miles of grueling washed out, washboard roads to reach the trailhead that led to Tassajara Zen Mountain Center in the Ventana wilderness area of the Los Padres mountains, southeast of Carmel. Then we hiked for two days to reach Tassajara, the oldest Japanese Buddhist Zen monastery in the United States.

The monastery lived by a code of silence at all times, with the exception of dinner.

The peacefulness of the place gave me the first peace I had felt since leaving BYU. A comforting quietness allowed me to take full, deep breaths.

The monks made and sold homemade bread. The property featured incredible hot springs with private baths. A river nearby supplied cold soaks. I was startled to discover no one wore clothes or bathing suits in the hot springs. Before entering the area, I shyly removed my clothing, trying to act like I had done this many times before.

I took a deep breath and walked through the gate. Naked people everywhere were soaking up the sun, men and women separated by an old wooden fence with spaces between the slats like a kid before braces. I had never seen adults naked and tried not to stare. Gradually, I relaxed and enjoyed the rays warming my first-ever, publicly nude body.

Leaving the hot springs, we continued our hike back to Carmel through the Los Padres Mountains. Eventually, we came to an incredible waterfall with a green-blue pool at the bottom. People took off their clothing and jumped in. I joined them, letting out a scream when I hit the water. It was freezing! I quickly swam to the side and pulled myself up out of the pool. Lying there in the sun, right in front of me, was a naked man. Inadvertently, my head came up level with his privates. I got a very good, live, close-up of his penis. It pretty much looked like the pictures in the book my BYU therapist had given me, but contrary to his belief, it didn't scare me.

The women on this trip were easy to be around and were highly accomplished. I enjoyed getting to know them and was struck by how human and kind and smart they were. Late into the night, we discussed politics, religion, and life experiences. They talked about issues I had never discussed firsthand, like about a woman's right to choose an abortion. It made sense to me that a woman had the right to choose, and yet, I was conflicted about the rights of the fetus. When one of them said, "But what about medical necessity, like if the pregnancy could risk the life of the mother?" The more they discussed this, the more confused I became. I realized the right to choose was not as cut and dry as I had been taught. But what I really appreciated was the fact that they were able to voice their true opinions. I quietly sat and soaked it all in.

One day, when one of the gals seemed to be struggling physically as we hiked up a steep incline, they slowed their pace, encouraging her forward. We hiked, played, and worked as a cohesive group. Lesbian or not, these were the type of people I wanted to have in my life. They made me feel normal for the first time since I could remember.

I spent a lot of time talking with one woman in particular. Leslie Thompson was six years older than me, and we had heartfelt conversations about playing sports and about how much we both loved being on a team. We spoke about the coaches who had impacted us the most, and about the mindset necessary to be a successful athlete.

Leslie also shared a story with me about her deepest struggle, which happened when she sustained a serious injury while playing field hockey in college. Even now, I could see the disappointment on her face. She explained to me that many of the skills I acquired as an athlete, I would one day use to create success in my life - especially the skill of never giving up.

As I lay in my sleeping bag at night, while trying not to focus on the hard ground, I thought about how the things I had learned by playing sports could help me to have a happy, good life - even if I wasn't in the Mormon Church.

I didn't talk about BYU because it was still too painful, but if I had, I am certain she would have been sympathetic and understanding. Leslie was funny, kind, and smart. I couldn't help but notice her jet black, wavy hair, her almond-shaped hazel eyes, her olive skin, and the little dark freckles sprinkling her nose. She was quick to smile, and had a gentle presence that felt familiar and comfortable to me.

I knew Leslie wouldn't be interested in someone my age, and quite honestly, I was not looking. I couldn't imagine opening my heart to anyone - friend or lover. My Mormon friends weren't talking to me, and I had lost Sam.

After the trip, Leslie continued to call me and we got together often, just as friends. I began sharing pieces of my struggle with her, and she was the first person to listen to me without trying to convince me one way or the other. Without realizing it, I began to trust her, and her friendship became important to me. I felt like she was the only real friend I had.

One night after a movie, I told her about BYU. I shared my

heartache about Sam, and I told her I had been formally expelled, expectantly waiting for her reaction. Kindly, she reached forward and pulled me into her arms. Gently hugging me, she told me she was so sorry I had gone through something so painful and difficult. I didn't realize how rigidly I was holding myself until I felt myself breathe in her arms, and my body started to relax. I couldn't believe she didn't judge me.

One weekend, she invited me to the Bay Area for a water skiing trip with one of her old tennis coaches. We stayed at her parent's house. Her parents were charming, and I instantly hit it off with her younger brother, David. After we arrived, we all went out for a delicious dinner and then returned home to go to bed early since we would be getting up at six the next morning to go up to the lake.

We carried our bags into Leslie's old room and each claimed one of the two single beds. Hers was closest to the window. Shyly, I got into my pajamas and crawled into bed, looking the other way as Leslie did the same. Even though we had spent time together and had talked a lot on the phone, we were usually with others, or out in public. Sharing the privacy of a bedroom seemed like a big step, not in terms of romance but just in the sense of being at ease with each other.

I expected Leslie to turn out the light; instead, she rolled up on her elbow and started a conversation that lasted late into the night. I liked many things about her, including the fact that we could dive into serious conversation then burst out laughing. Just as I was starting to feel sleepy, Leslie got out of bed and came over to me. She sat on the edge of my bed, bent down, and kissed me softly.

Her kiss took me by surprise. I didn't know she felt like that about me, and I hadn't let myself go there either. Closing myself off to Sam closed me off to any thought of love with someone else. Leslie kissed me again, this time more passionately. I felt that familiar tingle as she slid in beside me and began touching me. I pulled back, looking deeply in her eyes.

Softly, she smiled.

In that moment, I realized I was falling in love with her. Slowly, she kissed my neck, while sliding my pajamas off my shoulder. I felt myself opening, giving myself to her completely, and for the first time ever, my church, my religion, and my family were completely out of my mind.

It felt natural to fall in love with Leslie, and eventually we made plans to live together in El Cerrito, on the Berkeley line across the bay from San Francisco. My parents were angry, and we had a horrible disagreement. They banned Leslie from their home and I hardly saw them over the next two years.

Leslie and I were a great match. She was a high school coach, and I was studying business at Cal State Hayward and working in an accounting firm. During the day, we worked or played, and at night, we passionately made love into the wee hours of the morning. Patiently, she taught me how to be a woman, a passionate lover, and an adult.

We had a healthy, monogamous relationship, and constantly interacted with her family. They accepted us exactly as they did their other two children and their spouses. We enjoyed family dinners together, spent countless hours working in her parent's yard, and often went over just to hang out and watch TV.

Spending time with family had always been so important to me, and it was equally important to Leslie. No alcohol, no drugs, no all-night parties. I was living the moral life I had been taught to live, with one small exception: I was living it alongside a woman I loved.

I bought a baby blue VW Super Beetle for the commute down to Cal State Hayward. On the weekends, and some weeknights, Leslie and I would tie our sailboards on top of the car and head for the San Francisco Bay. I will never forget driving down the freeway, looking at the sparkling water in the Bay, with the boards rocking my VW bug, as if we were flying.

Occasionally, I would speak to my parents by phone. After the calls, days of guilt would set in. I hid it from Leslie because I didn't want her to question my commitment to her, or maybe I didn't want to think about what the guilt might cause me to do. I began to exercise heavily and run a lot to quiet my concerns.

Sailboarding became my escape from the mounting sense that the life I was living was very wrong. I could lose myself on my board, holding on with all of my might as I raced across the Bay, San Francisco at my back, the wind in my hair, sun on my face, and the taste of salt in my mouth. When I ran, it was to outrun my thoughts. When I was on the sailboard, the thoughts didn't even show up.

My parents moved to Idaho Falls, Idaho. I missed my family very much, and although we didn't visit, the idea of them being further away made me long for them even more. I ached to see my younger brothers and sisters, especially my little sister Bonnie who was growing up without me.

Several months after my parents moved to Idaho Falls, Mom called and invited Leslie and me to come for a visit. I was shocked, and grateful. I burst into tears when I hung up the phone. My family and Leslie, the people I loved most in the world, would finally get to know each other. I didn't let my thoughts go further than that because it felt so good to be going home with Leslie, and to be with my family.

We loaded our backpacks and flew to Idaho Falls. Nervously, we walked off the plane into the welcoming arms of both my parents. I appreciated them including Leslie in the hugs, knowing it was difficult for them, especially for Mom. Their choice to be with me, even if it meant me being with the woman I loved, felt good in a way I hadn't known from them in a very long time.

The visit with my family went well. I soaked up the joy of family life and took in the wonder of my brothers and sisters - the familiar sound of everyone talking during dinner, the laughter as we played games at the kitchen table late into the night, and my mom's homemade cooking. It felt good to be back home, and to have Leslie be a part of my family, I missed them even more than I realized. Leslie and I headed out on a four-day hike into the Alaska Basin in the Tetons, which completed our trip perfectly.

Even though the trip home went well, I noticed the old dread returning once we got back to California. It claimed more and more of my attention. There was no doubt I loved Leslie, yet my love for her was being compromised by a growing sense that I was doing something wrong and by a pull I felt toward Mom for the tough choice she had made to invite Leslie and me to visit. This was a hard choice she had made, to place her love for me over her own disapproval of the way I was living my life.

At about the same time, a guy at work showed interest in me. He laid it on thick with gifts, flowers and attention. He turned out to be the kind of guy to stay away from, but his advances reminded me that being with a man was still a possibility. That, along with my gnawing guilt over being lesbian, conspired to make me open to my mom's next desperate plea.

A couple of months after we returned from Idaho Falls, Mom called and begged me to try the church one more time. "There has to be an answer out there," she said.

I heard the pain in her voice, the anguish. She was trying to save her daughter from going to hell, and I didn't want to go there, either. I was twenty-one years old, but the girl in me craved her mother's approval and wanted to relieve her mother's torture. If there was a cure for me then I'd make one last try at being a man-loving woman.

I left Leslie and broke both of our hearts.

Chapter 25
One More Try At Normal

My decision to leave Leslie thrilled my parents. It left me desolate. I willed myself to stuff my sorrow and live straight as a Mormon woman.

Since Idaho Falls didn't offer me what I wanted educationally, Dad suggested I move to Salt Lake City and attend the University of Utah, his alma mater. My grandparents and other relatives were nearby and I could visit with them anytime. I would live with my mother's parents in Bountiful while I got my feet on the ground, and I would be only a couple of miles away from Mom's sister, Mary Ann. Besides, Grams lived only thirty miles away in Salt Lake City.

I arrived in Utah, an adult woman who had left her female lover to win the approval of her family, church and God - and hopefully overcome her sinful ways. The move tumbled me into a dark depression that lasted for months.

Every day I would wake up in a black pit, force myself forward, and go through the motions of my resolve to be good and straight. I missed Leslie with all of my heart, and the safe, normal life we had created. I returned to church as an active member. I fasted, prayed, read my scriptures, and did whatever was necessary to make God happy. I felt like a fish swimming on the outside of the tank, flapping its fins in a useless effort to get back in. I wouldn't give up. This *had* to work.

I didn't have the money to start school, so I began earning it by setting up computer systems for individual clients and businesses. My outlook improved, I made some friends, and started playing city league softball and basketball.

For two years, I worked hard, went to church, dated nice guys and resisted thoughts of women. To cope, I exercised like mad and kept insanely busy. Eventually a man from church hired me to computerize oil jobbers around the country.

My Grams became my lifeline to feeling loved and being normal. By this time, I was living in an apartment at the base of Big and Little Cottonwood Canyons, and she lived only a couple of miles away. Her house was an easy stop for yummy dinners and warm, loving arms.

One night, Grams and I went to dinner and a movie. When we returned to her house, she invited me in to talk for a while. I could tell she had something on her mind, and it put me on alert. As she unlocked the door, I could smell the familiar scent of dried flowers and homemade wheat bread. She offered to make me some toast with homemade strawberry jam, an irresistible treat. She poured us some apple juice, and we sat down at her kitchen table with our toast. Over the years, we had spent many hours at that table, talking and laughing late into the night.

Grams reached over and took me by the hand. "Marnie, why were you sent home from BYU?"

I looked at her and didn't move.

She said, "Marn, I love you with all of my heart and there is nothing you could ever do that would change that."

I wanted to fall into her arms and sob out the whole story. I knew she would wrap her arms around me, I knew she would stroke my head and say that sometimes we just don't know why things happen the way they do, and I knew she would love me just the same. And more than anything, I wanted my Grams, who I loved and trusted, to tell me it was going to be okay, that it was all going to work out.

I looked into her loving eyes, framed by those beloved laugh lines. Tears filled my eyes, then I turned away. My parents had asked me specifically to not say anything about BYU to Grams. They said it was private and other family members did not need to know. I had promised them I would not tell her, or anyone else.

Grams held on to my hand, and asked again. I stood up and said, "Grams, I'm sorry but I can't tell you."

I pulled my hand out of hers and left. I got in my car and drove away from the one person whose arms would have held me without judgment while I cried, the person who could have loved me when I couldn't love myself. A deep, gut-wrenching cry spread from my chest through my body, and gushed out in loud sobs. I was a hostage to my secret, locked by a promise not to tell.

Chapter 26
The F's

I was 23 years old and I finally had enough money to enroll at the University of Utah. My life was adequately together so that I could succeed at being a student and work on the side. I left my job computerizing oil jobbers and returned to freelancing. I was excited about returning to school with a double major in Finance and Pre-Med.

On my application to Cal State Hayward years before, when I was living with Leslie, I didn't include BYU on my application. Pretending it never happened seemed safer than including it. I didn't want to risk not being accepted because I had been expelled from BYU.

But here I was in Utah, the same state as BYU. Surely someone would find out. So I decided to include BYU on my application. The only thing I needed was my transcripts; I couldn't help but wonder what came up when they typed my name into their computer. One afternoon, I mustered the courage to call, gave them my name, and asked for my transcripts. I was told the request had to be in writing, so I complied. But rather than have them sent to the University of Utah, I requested them to be sent to me, just in case there were any surprises.

About two weeks later, an envelope with the shiny BYU lettering arrived. I walked slowly into the house and sat down at my kitchen table, holding the envelope. It felt like a time bomb in my hand. Again, I felt a knot in my belly as the memories flooded over me. Whatever happened to Sam?

Slowly, I tore open the envelope and slid out the paper. My

hands were trembling as if it were once again the morning the Head of Standards declared me unfit for BYU and the entire state of Utah.

I unfolded the paper, not believing what I saw. Rather than the Withdrawals the Head of Standards had promised me as grades for my classes, I had "Failures." Every single class showed an "F". I laid my head on the table and cried bitter tears. Would this ever be over? How would I ever get into the U?

I wondered if they had given Sam Failures, too. Several days later I dug out my old BYU phone book and called her to find out. My heart was pounding.

Her mother answered the phone. I said, "Hello, I am an old friend of Sam's from BYU. Could I speak with her?"

Her voice became tense. "Who is this?"

"Marnie Freeman," I said. I couldn't lie.

She hung up the phone.

I called back. "Don't call here again," she said, slamming down the phone a second time.

I called a third time, then a fourth. She hung up each time.

I sat there staring at the phone. It rang.

"Hello," I said.

"You have no idea what amazing things have happened for Sam," said her mother. "This could ruin everything."

"I don't want to hurt Sam," I said. "I have one simple question that I need answered."

"What," she asked.

"Did Sam receive W's for her classes at BYU?" I asked.

"Yes," she said. "Sam returned to BYU the next semester."

She then apologized for hanging up on me. I told her I understood. She asked me to promise to never call Sam again. I agreed and kept my promise.

I felt I needed help on this one. I couldn't get my F's changed to W's on my own. I called my parents to tell them about my transcripts from BYU. I told them Sam had received Withdrawals. They told me to talk with my Bishop and see if there was something he could do to help me. I made an appointment.

As hard as I tried to get her out of my mind, thoughts of Sam came flooding back. I couldn't help but think about the last night we spent together, the loving tenderness I felt while lying next to her. Feelings I had worked so hard to forget were still deep in my heart. I found it difficult to breathe, and I felt as raw as the day I was expelled from BYU.

I explained to the Bishop that I had gone to BYU, had some issues, and left early. "The Head of Standards told me I would receive Withdrawals in all my classes, but instead I received Failures." I showed him the transcript.

"I have a good friend at BYU," he said. "Give me a copy and I will look into it."

The Bishop called me a couple of weeks later and asked me to meet with him. As he ushered me to a chair, I couldn't tell by the look on his face if the news was good or bad.

"There is a solution," he said, "but we will have to go through a process."

"A process," I thought. "Okay, I can jump through hoops."

"Are you currently in good standing with the church?" he asked.

"Yes, I am a worthy member of the church," I said.

He outlined the process. "I must write a letter on your behalf," he said. "The Stake President must interview you and write a letter on your behalf. Your parents must write a letter on your behalf, and you must also write a letter stating you regret your actions, you know they were a mistake, and you must apologize.

Hopefully we will get these grades reversed."

"Okay," I said. "Who do I write the letter to?"

"Write it to Brother Richard Stewart, the Director of Admissions," he said. My mouth went dry. Richard Stewart was the Head of Standards when I was at BYU, now the Director of Admissions. He was the man who had me sit in shame for weeks in front of his desk, the same man who expelled me and said he hoped I would never set foot in Utah again, the same man who promised me Withdrawals. Richard Stewart would be the one receiving all of our letters. He would be the one to receive my letter of apology. He would be the one to decide if my F's would become W's.

I kept this information to myself. Numbly, I shook the Bishop's hand and drove to my apartment.

Within a few weeks, the Bishop and my parents had written their letters, and the Stake President had interviewed me and written his letter. My letter was the only one left to be written. They were all to be sent together, as a package.

I tried to write my letter at least twenty times. Each attempt sent me down a rabbit hole that left me upset at the injustice, angry over the broken promise, and demoralized by the need to grovel for what was rightly mine - particularly to the very man who had treated me so unjustly. I had never felt so powerless.

I screamed, "This is not right!"

Screaming felt good but didn't get the job done. So I put myself in a zone of numbness and began writing.

I wrote down all the things I knew Richard Stewart would want to hear. I knew the importance he put on humiliation, judgment, unkindness, and disrespect. I knew he wanted me to be deeply sorry for who I was and what I had done. I knew he wanted me to own the fact that my actions were wrong and an abomination before God. I knew I had to say I was deeply sorry for all the people I had impacted and hurt, and that my greatest hope was to be worthy of a temple marriage. I knew I had to apologize to him directly, and ask for him to find forgiveness in his heart. I knew I had to say I had repented of my sins, that God had forgiven me, and that I no longer had feelings for women.

For the first time, I told a lie about my true feelings. I lied in order to receive the W's I had been promised. This was highly ironic, since it had been my commitment to honesty that got me expelled in the first place. Not only did I lie, I betrayed myself.

A month went by with no response. I called my Bishop who said he would make a call to see how things were coming. "Try not to worry," he added.

A couple of weeks later, a shiny BYU envelope was delivered to my mailbox. Nervously, I walked into my apartment and sat down at the kitchen table, with the envelope in my hand. I had been replaying my last days at BYU for weeks, my last days with Sam. If the envelope held the W's I needed, I hoped to move on.

The "F's"

I opened the envelope and unfolded the transcript. There were W's where the F's had been. I jumped up, screamed with relief, and once and for all, put BYU behind me.

University of Utah, here I come!

Chapter 27
My Lowest Point and the Turning Point

My apartment was on the boundary line of a different ward, and so I became a new member of a young adult ward for unmarried Mormons ages 18-30. These wards were organized just like regular wards, except the Bishopric - the Bishop and his counselors - were adults from outside wards. The rest of the leadership and teaching positions were filled by the young adults within the ward. I was one of the teachers.

I liked my new Bishop immediately. Bishop Oakley seemed kind and smart, and his eyes sparkled with deep smile lines. Our ward had an abundance of church activities. We went skiing and hiking, hosted dances, often enjoyed dinners together, and, of course, there was always church on Sundays.

The unspoken idea was to keep all of the young adults as worthy members of the church by making sure we were too busy to go down the forbidden path of pre-marital sex. It was kind of like a holding tank until you were married.

One weekend, Bishop Oakley invited all of us to his cabin for an overnight ski trip. We had a blast fixing dinner together and playing games. I had made some good friends in the group, both women and men.

Before BYU, I had dated and kissed some great guys. Since arriving in Salt Lake, I had been dating, but I never let myself get to the point of kissing anyone. I told myself it wasn't like I was avoiding it; I just hadn't met any guys I felt like kissing.

That night in the cabin, as I looked around at the people who were in my group, I wondered who I could feel something for, and if it was actually possible for me to feel more than just dead inside. I had willed myself into feeling nothing for anyone. It was safer that way. Not feeling anything would keep me from going down the wrong path with the wrong gender.

As my eyes darted from person to person, it occurred to me that nothing had changed. I was still in the same place. I thought the guys were fun but felt nothing romantically toward any of them. So I looked at the women in the room. There was only one that I could possibly be interested in.

Her name was Danielle and she was one of the most straight-laced girls in our entire ward. She was accomplished, had a beautiful voice, and kept all the rules, which suited her well as our Relief Society President, the top female position in our ward. In a nutshell, Danielle would make the perfect Mormon wife. While imagining how horrified Danielle would be to know that, if I had to choose someone in the room, it would be her, I heard my name called. I jumped. It was my turn to play Pictionary™.

Danielle was holding a large white board in front of her, while people drew on the board. Her head poked out above the board and her knees were below it. As I walked up to choose my card and get my marker, something came over me. Call it stupid or call it funny, but instead of drawing what was on my card, I drew a naked body that fit the outline of Danielle's torso. I did it in such a way that nobody could tell what I was drawing until the end when I drew one last line that connected the body and added two large breasts. I stepped away.

At first no one made a sound, and then everybody burst into laughter. They couldn't hold it in. Even the Bishop laughed as he averted his eyes. Danielle was very thin, and I had intentionally drawn a large, voluptuous body, which made everyone laugh even more.

Danielle hadn't been watching me draw, so when everyone began laughing she looked from side to side to see what was so funny, then she looked down at the white board.

"Marnie!!!!" Danielle screamed my name in horror.

I joined in the laughter, although mine had an edge to it that the others would never know.

Later, as everyone was getting ready for bed, I stopped to talk to the Bishop in the kitchen. He didn't mention my Pictionary™ prank. Instead, he asked me about school and how things were going. He seemed genuinely interested and very nice. I was glad to be in his ward.

My brother, Rohn, had just come home from his two year mission in Indiana, where he proselytized for the Mormon Church, and he'd asked to move in with me. Rohn was two years younger than me, and we had always been the best of friends. We had spent all of our growing up years hanging out together with our circle of friends. I was overjoyed that he would be moving in with me.

One day, about a month after Rohn moved in, he came rushing into our apartment with Grams following behind. I saw the stress on his face.

"I split Gram's head open," he said, breathless. "We need to take her to the hospital."

In the background I heard Grams say, "I am not going to the hospital!"

As she came through the door, I saw rivulets of blood running down her face and over her ears. Stunned, I looked at my brother and asked, "What happened!?"

"We were golfing," he explained. "Grams had hit her ball into the rough and was standing next to it, way over to the right. I hit my ball and it sliced to the right, too." Rohn took a breath and continued. "I yelled 'Fore! Fore Grams, Fore!!!' But she was too far away to hear me and my ball came straight down on her head."

He told me that after the ball hit Grams, she spun slowly in a circle twice, then fell to the ground.

Rohn ran over to her and found her sitting there, dazed. "What happened?" she asked.

Sheepishly, Rohn answered "My ball hit you on the head, Grams."

Even with blood running down her face, she burst into laughter, and said, "Rohn! I can't believe it!"

I examined her head and said, "Grams, you need stitches. We have to go to the hospital."

She was a surgical nurse at St. Marks. She looked me dead in the eye and said, "I am *not* going to the hospital, and you guys are going to fix me up."

I was doing Pre-Med at the U, but I hadn't been anywhere near a hospital at that point. The closest thing to working on humans I had experienced was in the cadaver lab. Grams took control. She made a list and told Rohn what to get at the drugstore. Then she ordered me to go get a clean razor blade.

Grams and I went into the bathroom while Rohn drove to the pharmacy. It was surreal scrubbing blood out of my Grams' strawberry blonde hair. I got a cotton ball and wiped the blood out of her right ear. Once most of the blood was cleaned up, she told me to shave the top of her head.

"Are you sure, Grams?" I asked, incredulously.

She gave me the look that said, *"Do it,"* and I did.

By the time Rohn got back, Grams looked like one of those monks who shave the hair off the top of their heads, but leave the rest. When Rohn walked in, we all burst into laughter.

I cleaned out the gash, steri-stripped it back together, and off she went. The story became one of our favorites, recounted by Grams at many family gatherings.

Our apartment sat back in the trees, along a little stream. Rohn and I would often sit outside, listening to the water and watching the ducks. One warm, summer evening I walked over to the trash bin to throw away my garbage. On the way back, two gals sitting on the steps said hello to me. As I walked over to them, I realized they were a couple. I froze in my tracks, feeling my throat tighten. They told me they had graduated from college, played college softball, and had moved in about six months earlier. We talked for a little bit and I said I needed to get going. They said they would love to hang out with me some time and asked if I would like to play on their city softball team. Realizing I would love to play on their softball team, I made a quick exit, saying I would see them some other time.

On my way back to my apartment, I decided I would do everything to avoid them.

The pain of my experience at BYU was great enough to make me not want to repeat it. I willed myself to think about anything other than women, and if that didn't work, I would exercise until I was too exhausted to think about anything at all.

But meeting Deb and Kaitlin that night opened the floodgates of feelings once more and forced me to face the truth that the fasting and prayer, my self-control, being busy all the time, teaching, and spending time with my friends had done nothing to change me. Yet I wasn't going to give up. I had made a commitment to being a worthy Mormon and I would stick to it.

In fact, I would step it up. I would put myself on a higher plane of accountability, and the way to do that would be to confess to Bishop Oakley. I needed to admit and receive forgiveness for my past. So, I set up a time to meet with him.

I recounted the headlines of my relationships with women, including Sam and Leslie. Under my breath, I said I had not had sex with a man, hoping that would count for something. His face told me he was shocked, but he was extremely kind about it.

"What's your intention now?" he asked.

"I want to overcome my feelings," I said, "but they still seem as strong as before."

"Are you currently engaged in any immoral activity?" he asked.

"No," I said.

He gave me a wide smile and said, "Marnie, I know there is an answer out there somewhere. With my financial resources and your willingness to change, I know we can find the solution."

I had never considered that money could buy my answer, but I had to admit it was the best offer I'd heard from anyone since this whole thing began. A ray of hope lit my darkness.

"I will call you in two weeks to let you know what I find," he said.

I felt like I was on a cloud as I drove home. The lightness was intoxicating. Someone was finally going to help me. I could hardly wait for the two weeks to pass so I could start the process, whatever it would be.

Two weeks went by and I didn't hear anything. I knew he would call me, so I waited another week. On the Sunday of the third week, I walked up to him at church to shake his hand, hoping that his seeing me would remind him he had news for me. It didn't work.

I made every excuse in the book for him. I debated about calling him, but didn't. I'm not sure if I wasn't wanting to rush him or if I didn't want to know his answer.

I was 24-years old, waiting by the phone like I was 16, waiting for my Bishop to free me from my Lesbian self. He was my last hope.

I gave him another week and left a message for him to call me. Nothing. A couple of days later I called again. He didn't respond. I was beginning to feel desperate. I called and left a message at his house, with no call back. I called two more times and left messages before I admitted to myself that he had no answer for me.

There was no answer.

The letdown felt more than I could bear. It was a Friday, and I stayed up late into the night, thinking. I couldn't eat; I just sat in my bed, thinking. I fell asleep for a few hours, then continued thinking through Saturday. My thoughts ran in this loop: *There is no answer. There is no hope for me. I cannot change who I am. I cannot be a lesbian.*

The more my thoughts twirled in my brain, the more depressed I became.

My brother loved guns and had several in his bedroom. Late Saturday night, I opened the door to his room and picked up the handgun he kept loaded in case someone broke into our apartment. It felt heavy as I picked it up, and the steel of the barrel felt cold against my clammy hand.

I walked back into my room and shut the door, returning to my bed where I had been sitting for the last twelve hours. Holding the gun in my lap, I rocked back and forth, replaying the last four years of my life. Several hours passed.

I was done. I could not handle it anymore. I raised the gun to my head, placing the barrel against my right temple. It felt slippery because I was drenched in sweat. I clenched my teeth, and I could hear a deep sound coming from my throat. I clenched harder, squeezing my eyes tightly shut. My arm was shaking. Time moved as if in slow motion. I was finished. I could not fight any longer.

I squeezed the handle of the gun and placed my finger on the trigger, beginning to pull it back. I was grinding my teeth with such pressure it felt like they were going to shatter.

And then, in an instant, I saw a vision of my mother. In it, my mother was kneeling with her arms draped over my coffin, sobbing. I had destroyed my mother's life.

In that split second, I froze. Slowly, I released the trigger, hearing a click as it went back into its resting place. I gulped in deep breaths of air, lowered the gun, and shook, as sobs wracked my body.

For the first time, I understood that Mom would rather have me alive and gay than dead.

I sobbed through the night about the Mormon life I had to leave behind - the people, my family, the clear lines, the caring community, the safety, and the pre-set path. I had worked so hard to keep it together, but now I understood it was an impossible undertaking. Hope of being Mormon and gay moved out of my heart, and a haunting emptiness moved in.

You don't get to be Mormon and a lesbian, even if you were born being both.

Finally, early in the morning hours, I fell into a deep sleep. When I awoke, I had that brief moment of not remembering anything, then the heaviness returned. As I crawled out of bed, I felt the weight of what lay ahead. I needed time to figure out what I was going to do.

The following week, I went through the motions of life. The next weekend, I went to Bear Lake with our young adult ward for an overnight water ski trip. I had helped plan the trip and felt responsible to see it through. I had mapped a bike route through the Bear River Mountains, a branch of the Wasatch Range, for those who wanted to bike to the cabin rather than drive.

Early Saturday morning, twelve of us set out on bikes, with a support van following. There were five girls and seven guys. The sky was robin's egg blue, without a single cloud. The air was crisp and fresh. As I got on my bike, I took a deep breath. Within thirty minutes of pedaling, I felt my body start to relax, the relentless sorrow I carried began to dissipate.

We started in Riverside, rode up around the tip of the mountain, through Mendon, across Cache Valley, and began our difficult climb up Logan canyon. The canyon rose to an elevation of 7,800 feet after a vertical climb of about 2,900 feet. Just beyond the summit was a steep road descending into Bear Lake Valley.

As we began the steepest part of our climb, it became clear that not everyone was going to make it. It was the toughest ride I had ever attempted. I had ridden Provo canyon when I was at BYU and had ridden Big and Little Cottonwood Canyons, but nothing had felt quite as steep as this. I felt so tortured inside, I welcomed this grueling challenge; I wanted the physical punishment.

Two girls peeled off, and the van picked them up. Another mile, and we lost two of the guys. Slowly, we continued to climb, each taking our turn at the lead. Soon, four of us pulled ahead - Clint, Shawn, a guy I didn't know well, and me. I had dated Clint several times. He was a super nice guy and he was really athletic, but I never felt anything more for him than friendship. We rode together, taking turns in the lead, and continued to climb.

Memories of having held the gun to my head played like a movie in my mind. I pedaled hard. What was I going to do? I pedaled harder. I wasn't going to try and be somebody else anymore. I clenched my teeth and pedaled even harder than before. I was a failure. I was a disappointment. And most importantly, I would never be normal. Every muscle in my legs burned; still, I pedaled harder.

As we climbed, my lungs began to burn. I was not going to quit. This climb would not beat me. I noticed there were just three riders now, Clint, Shawn and me. We continued to climb. Carloads of people from our ward passed us, honking and waving as they went by, cheering us on.

Adrenaline and a steely resolve pushed me forward. Finally, Shawn said, "I'm done," and pulled to the side. For a moment I faltered. I had been certain the three of us would make it to the finish. Shawn saw me hesitate and immediately encouraged me to keep going.

As we neared the summit, every muscle in my body was screaming to quit. Clint and I were both standing as we pumped, using our weight to push down the next pedal. As we climbed through the Aspen trees, I remembered the many times Mom took us to Bear Lake when we were young and lived in Mendon. My parents owned a lot on the lake, and we went there three or four times a week during the summers. I remembered making rafts out of inner tubes with Kate, Rohn, and George, and basking in the hot sun baring down on the lake.

As I reached the peak of the pass, I was physically and emotionally exhausted. The ride had become more than a strenuous day on a bike pushing me beyond my physical capacity; I was riding for my life, the old life that I had to leave behind, and the new life I had to face. A sense of peace washed over me as I realized I had to leave the church. There would be no more living a life that was half way for me. I would no longer be a Mormon and try not to be a lesbian, and I would no longer be a lesbian while trying to be Mormon.

I needed to be me - a lesbian woman.

Saturday evening, I was sitting on the deck of the cabin looking out at the lake, listening to the gentle breeze through the quaking aspen. Clint came up and sat down by me. I saw a certain look in his eye.

He said, "I think we should start seeing each other."

I looked at him and said, "I'm so sorry Clint, I can't. But thank you for asking." I got up and walked away.

I went to see Bishop Oakley one last time, not to seek an answer, but to give him mine. He never said a word about not calling me back. I told him I needed to accept who I was and follow my heart.

He said, "I'm sad to hear that." Then he added, "If you choose to live this life, I ask that you not socialize with the women of the church. You have too much power over many of them. When you were a teacher, it was a good thing. Now, I think you could pull some of them away with you. I ask that you not."

I never went back to church again.

Chapter 28
I Switch Gears

I walked over to Deb and Kaitlin's apartment and told them I'd love to play softball with them. I started dating one of the girls on my softball team, a Claims Adjuster from Michigan. We enjoyed a lot of the same things and eventually moved in together. I was not in love with her but we had a lot of fun. She was the first in a string of turn-style relationships that usually lasted about two years. The women were as emotionally unavailable as I was. Sometimes I left first, sometimes they did. I did not believe the relationships could or should last. After all, they were wrong in the eyes of God, so obviously, they were doomed to fail.

One night, Grams invited me over for dinner. She made one of my favorite meals, chicken cordon bleu, creamy mashed potatoes, and a fresh salad. As usual, we laughed as we talked about old memories. With each memory, she reached out and touched my hand, or kiddingly pushed my shoulder as she recounted some of the naughty things I'd done.

As I watched her laugh, my heart filled with incredible love. Whenever I spent time with her, I felt as though love radiated from every cell of her body, pure unconditional love.

It was getting late, and I sat back in my seat saying I probably needed to go. Grams looked at me and said, "I need to tell you something. Your mom and dad spoke with me and told me why you were expelled from BYU." My heart sank. I felt badly that it had taken so long for her to know, and I felt badly that I hadn't shared this with her myself. She deserved better from me.

I didn't want to betray my parents, but I wanted to explain to her that they had asked me not to tell her. I wanted to tell her I loved and trusted her, and that I was so sorry I hadn't been truthful with her and hadn't told her myself.

I wanted to tell her all that, but I couldn't get the words out.

She reached over and took my hand, with tears in her eyes, and said: "Marnie, this does not change anything. I love you as much as I always have, and I always will. I told your Mom and Dad to let it be. I told them to love you unconditionally, and to leave this up to the Lord, that there are some things we just don't understand."

I felt my throat tighten as tears filled my eyes. I looked at her and said, "Thanks Grams." She took me in her arms and hugged me tightly. With warmth in my heart, I kissed her on the cheek, thanked her again and left.

I was so thankful she finally knew.

I was still self-employed setting up computer systems while enrolled at the U. A Salt Lake City Chinese Medicine Clinic hired me to install a new accounting and computer system, a job that lasted about six months. When I walked through the doors of the clinic for the first time, I was swept away by the aromas, the herbs, and the Chinese philosophy of healing. I had never experienced anything like it.

The office manager, Jenna, gave me a tour, while explaining their work and how it flowed. She took me to the back of the clinic to meet the owner, Dr. Eagon. We walked into a large room filled with hundreds of gallon-sized jars, each filled with herbs, leaves, seeds, sticks and minerals. I was fascinated by the bottles of liniments and tinctures, and intrigued by the formulations written in Chinese characters.

Jenna touched my shoulder to catch my attention and introduced me to Dr. Eagon.

"This is the most amazing thing I have ever seen," I said.

He smiled. "Have you ever been treated with Chinese Medicine?" he asked.

"No," I said. "I've never even heard of Chinese medicine."

One day while I was installing his clinic's computer system, a patient cancelled at the last minute. Dr. Eagon asked me if I would like a treatment. Without hesitation, I agreed. I was so curious about everything he was doing.

I explained to him that I had bad knees from all the years of having played basketball and having run so much. I had been going to physical therapy for the last six months and had not shown any improvement. In fact, a week earlier, my doctor had told me there was likely nothing to be done to relieve my knee pain.

Slowly, Dr. Eagon ran his hand over my knees. He had me flex and extend them and then said he felt he could help me. After three treatments my knees were 80% better. I was impressed. The positive results made me want to learn more. I asked him if there was anything I could read about Chinese Medicine. He loaned me a book called, *The Essentials of Acupuncture.*

The book filled me with questions. It was the first time I had ever heard of healing organs, instead of removing them when they were not working properly. Little did I know this book would be the beginning of another major change in my life.

Once my work at the clinic was complete, I didn't want to leave; Chinese Medicine was calling me. I wondered if a person had to go to China to study Chinese Medicine. Dr. Eagon told me there were twelve schools in the U.S. I ordered catalogs from each school and narrowed my choices down to four: The Oregon College of Oriental Medicine (OCOM) in Portland; Bastyr College in Seattle; and two schools in New Mexico. I had decided Chinese medicine would be my new path.

Next, I went on a couple of road trips to visit each school, looking for the one with the most rigorous internal medicine program. I observed a day of teaching at each school and studied the class requirements. I felt OCOM had the best program for me. I interviewed with the Dean of Admissions and the school president. As I drove through the Columbia River Gorge on my way back to Salt Lake City, I knew Portland was where I wanted to go to school.

Back at the University of Utah, I made an appointment to see Madeline, my Medical Advisor.

"I am going to study Chinese Medicine," I told her. Madeline was always friendly and had consistently been a big help to me. But my words turned her smile upside down.

"Nobody in the history of this school has ever done anything like that," she said. "It is ridiculous to even consider."

"Well, I will be the first," I said. I thanked her politely and left.

I graduated from the University of Utah in June of 1991. Then I spent the summer earning as much money as I could working in Dr. Eagon's Chinese Medicine Clinic, and left for Portland at the end of August. The twelve-hour drive gave me plenty of time to think.

I decided to turn over a new leaf in being honest about being a lesbian. I wouldn't try to hide it anymore. I would proudly be who I was.

As I drove into Hood River, Oregon, I saw people sail boarding on the river while the sun looked like a giant orange ball setting in the sky behind them. It was one of the most beautiful sites I had ever seen, and the peace I felt in that moment melted away any lingering doubts that I had made the right decision to move to Portland.

The morning after I arrived, classes began. The students gathered to meet each other. These would be the people I would study with for the next three years. They looked very different from the people in Salt Lake, less laced up and starched. Most of them were older than me and were coming back to school for a second career. I felt comfortable with them.

The instructor asked us each to tell a little bit about ourselves, our background, and where we were from. I remembered the promise I had made to myself the day before to live my life being who I truly was. When it was my turn, I stood up and said, "My name is Marnie Freeman. I just graduated from the University of Utah, and while I was driving out here yesterday, I decided that I am turning over a new leaf and being true to who I am. I am Lesbian."

Someone said "Right on!" and many of the people in the room clapped. I grinned, and as I sat down, my shoulders relaxed with a welcome relief. There would be no need to hide here.

The people in my class turned out to be some of the greatest people I had ever met. They were committed to healing, they were spiritual, they believed in making a difference in the world, and most importantly to me, they seemed to like me without judgment. To them, my sexuality was an afterthought, not the primary focus it had been for most everyone in my past. In the best way, they truly didn't care.

Finally being true to who I was, combined with my classes in Tai Qi, Qi Gong, and meditation, opened the door for me to re-think my spirituality. Since leaving the church four years earlier, I had been shut down, numb. I didn't have spirituality in my life because the one thing I still believed was that God could not possibly love me or want me. After all, I was living a life that contradicted all I understood Him to be.

For the first time ever, I let myself entertain the idea that a spiritual life as a lesbian woman was a possibility, and that maybe I could find my way to a loving, happy life after all.

Chapter 29
China

I graduated from the Oregon College of Oriental medicine in June of 1994 and immediately left for China to study at the Heilong Jiang College of Traditional Chinese Medicine. OCOM had sponsored this study trip to China, and people from other schools in the states joined our group, including people who were already in practice. My best friend Vickie, who I met at OCOM, also went on the trip.

My dad was kind enough to give me his air miles, so I left two days before the rest of the group. I landed in China after dark. I had learned to say *hello* and *thank you* in Chinese, along with a little medical terminology, but that was it. Luckily, I had a card with me showing the name of the "Rainbow Hotel" where I would meet up with the rest of the group. The hotel was an hour from the airport, and by the time I got there it was late. My body needed food.

I checked in, put my bag in my room, and found the hotel restaurant just as it was closing. Conversation stopped and all eyes turned to me as I walked in.

"Ni Hao (hello)," I said, bowing my head in respect.

"Ni Hao," they replied back.

In no time, twelve people surrounded me, trying to speak English. They located a local girl who spoke broken English. She asked what I wanted to eat. I was a vegetarian then and had no idea what to order. I pointed to the rice on someone else's plate. It was the only food I recognized. The group seemed disappointed with my food choice.

The young girl said, "We bring something very special, special hotel dish."

"Xie Xie, Xie Xie (thank you)," I said, bowing to each of the twelve. They giggled, saying "Xie Xie" back to me.

Hungrily, I waited for my meal. I loved Chinese food and couldn't wait for my special dish to arrive. When it was ready, the twelve filed in a line to my table. This had become an event. "Very special Chinese dish. Duck skin!"

My stomach twisted but I kept the smile on my face. Expectantly, they stood around my table waiting for me to take my first bite. I looked at my special dish, a deep pool of oil with a thick, soggy piece of duck skin floating on top. There was a small bit of meat attached to the skin, left by mistake. That's what I went for. I picked up my chopsticks and pulled the meat from the skin.

"Mmmm," I said, looking up at my observers. They laughed and said "Mmm" back. I covered the meat with as much rice as I could possibly get onto my chopsticks and popped it into my mouth.

It was my first meat in six years, but I couldn't really taste it because of the rice. The group remained, waiting for me to eat the duck skin. I picked up the whole thing with my chopsticks and tore off a bite with my teeth as the rest flopped back onto the plate, splashing oil on the table.

The skin was like a spongy hunk of fat and my gag reflex was on alert. Fortunately, once I took a bite, the twelve were satisfied and left. I ate my rice and escaped to my room.

I spent the following day walking around Beijing, looking for bookstores, in search of old Chinese medical texts. I found several treasures. The rest of the group would arrive that evening. I could not wait to see a familiar face, especially Vickie's.

I returned to the restaurant for dinner, better prepared to order.

"Gong Bao Jie Ding and Mifan, (Kung Pao Chicken and rice)," I said. The meal was delicious.

Then I heard Vickie calling my name, and I jumped up to hug her. I was so relieved to hear her voice. Patrick, our trip leader, introduced me to everyone in the group. I shook each person's hand and took particular notice of a lesbian couple from the East coast, as well as an attractive Eurasian woman from Maryland named Elana.

Vickie and Elana joined me at my table. They had become friends on the trip over. Elana had been practicing Chinese Medicine for many years and taught at the New England School of Acupuncture. I asked her questions about her practice, but she seemed uninterested in engaging in a conversation with me. I chalked it up to her being tired, but I did notice she was full of stories and laughter when she interacted with Vickie.

The following day we flew to Harbin, a city far to the north, on the Russian border, where we would spend all of our time working with Chinese Medicine doctors in four different hospitals, focusing on Internal Medicine.

We settled into our dorm rooms and went to bed early. Vickie and I shared a room together. The next morning we both woke with a start and jumped out of bed. The sun was high in the sky and we thought we had overslept, missing our morning rounds at the hospital. We threw on our clothes and put on our lab coats, opting not to wear the matching white hats. I grabbed my watch on the way out the door and did a double-take.

"Hey, Vickie," I said. "What time does your watch say?"

She looked at her watch and said, "Oh my god, it's only 6 AM!"

We were so far north that the sun had been up for hours. With our lab coats on, we fell back into our beds for one more hour of sleep.

We met the group for breakfast and walked over to the hospital together. It was a huge white building with lots of people bustling in and out. Vickie and I went to the Internal Medicine Department. We often saw 30 or 40 patients in the morning and the same number in the afternoon.

Unlike hospitals in the United States, we could send patients for an MRI or a CT scan - or any type of lab work - and they would be back in the afternoon, their test results in hand. No one had to wait for approval from an insurance company. We were able to diagnose and start treatment within the same day!

The weather in Harbin was very hot, so hot that streams of sweat would run down our legs and soak our socks. Our thick cotton lab coats extended past our knees. The first week, I wore professional clothing under my lab coat. The second week I wore shorts and a tank top. The third week I decided to wear only my bra and undies under my lab coat. No one could see my clothes anyway. Vickie did the same.

We worked hard by day and sat out on the tar roof of our dorm by night, drinking Bing Pi Jiu (cold beer) as we watched the sun set over the city. I was blissfully unaware of my sexuality and felt at peace.

We made good use of our weekends off. We explored Buddhist temples, mountains, villages, and lakes. The group spent a lot of time together. Elana continued to be cranky with me to the point that Vickie noticed.

"For some reason Elana does seem a little testy with you," she said.

I wondered what I had done to offend her, or if she just didn't like gay people.

At the end of our fourth week, the school loaded us onto buses, and we headed for Lianhua (Lotus Lake) outside of Da Qing city, the hunting land of the Mongolian Dorbod tribe, 100 miles northeast of Harbin. Vickie and I chose the seat in the very back of the van, and Elana joined us. By then, she had become somewhat warmer to me, but was still noticeably distant.

We were told the bus ride would take about two hours. Four hours later, we were still riding on a bumpy dirt road that gave us what felt like kidney punches every time we hit a deep pothole. It was hot and miserable.

Everybody in our group had dealt with occasional diarrhea, except me. My formula to health was drinking Qing Dao, a Chinese beer, every day and eating a clove of raw garlic to kill parasites anytime I ate off campus. However, by the sixth hour of the trip over the bumpy road, my turn came. I felt like I was going to explode.

Knowing I couldn't hold it any longer, I asked the driver to stop. The bus pulled over, letting everyone off for a break, the men on one side of the buses and the women on the other. There was no way I was going to have diarrhea in front of a group, so I jumped a ten-foot fence into a cornfield and took care of my business out there between the stalks.

We returned to the bus, and after a total of eleven hours of exhausting travel, we were told there had been a translation error. We had been driven to Da Qing oil fields up into Inner Mongolia rather than Da Qing City and Lotus Lake.

Finally, we pulled into a small village containing little mud dwellings. The residents of the village were short, brown-skinned people with creased eyes and deep smile lines. They surrounded me, wanting to touch my light skin and freckles. "Mei guo ren, Mei guo ren," they said, which meant "American person". They asked me if I would sell them my shirt, shoes, and watch. I declined their request with a smile and a bow.

We were directed to a hunting lodge half an hour away. Thankfully, there was room for us at the Lodge, a cement and log building nestled at the foot of a pristine lake. The sun was setting on a cloudless day.

Vickie and I put our things in our room and went to meet the others for dinner, which included heaps of tiny fried fish, piles of chicken feet, and other less-than-appetizing things I didn't recognize.

It was so damp there that the floors were slippery with moisture. Quickly, clouds came in and it began to rain. It rained so hard that Vickie went outside and stood under a drain spout, washing away the dust from the day. In what seemed like minutes, the clouds were gone, ushering in a crisp, clear night.

"Let's go swimming in the lake," I said, "in the moonlight."

Vickie wasn't up for it, so I went alone. I slipped off my clothes at the shore and waded into the cool water. The moon was deep yellow and enormous as it came up over the lake. I dove in and swam under water for as long as I could hold my breath. When I came up for air, wiping the water out of my eyes, I heard someone behind me. Turning, I was surprised to see Elana in the water to my left.

"Hello," I said, and swam in the opposite direction, not wanting to get in her space and preferring to protect my own. Of all people, I didn't want to be with her. I wanted the moon and the water to myself.

Elana swam over to me, stopping a couple feet away. The moonlight made her even more beautiful. She struck up a conversation, which surprised me. What had changed?

Elana dove under water and came up next to me. I stepped back. She took my hands in hers, bringing me under water with her. We circled together as we came up for air. She pulled me to her and put her mouth over mine. She wrapped her arms around my back, pulling me against her. I could feel her soft curves. Slow kisses became urgent as we passionately explored each other's bodies.

After a time, we went to shore, dressed and returned to the Lodge, each to our own rooms. I told Vickie what had transpired.

She laughed hysterically. "I'm not really surprised," she said. "I was starting to wonder if maybe that was why she was staying away from you."

I thought it was an odd way to treat someone you were attracted to, but it didn't really matter anymore. We enjoyed a passionate affair for the remainder of our time in China. I wasn't in love with Elana, but somehow on that moonlit night, my heart opened in a way it hadn't in a very long time. I allowed myself to feel something without worrying about getting hurt.

At the end of our residency at Heilongjiang and our time in Harbin, Vickie, Elana and I boarded a train in Beijing and traveled to Southern China. We took a boat down the Li River from Gui Lin to Yangshuo. Life on the river fascinated me and the beauty stole my heart.

Fishermen on long narrow boats used cormorant birds to catch fish. The Cormorant would see a fish, dive deep into the water and then surface. The fisherman would then hold the bird upside down while squeezing its neck until the fish fell out into his boat. The fish was food for the family and a source of income.

Villagers, on small boats piled high with vegetables, pulled up to larger boats to sell their produce. As we glided down this romantic river, I sat at the back of the boat, the wind blowing my hair as I listened to the bamboo along the river's edge sway back and forth, leaves rustling.

I may not have fallen in love with Elana, but I fell in love with China, and they both helped open my closed heart.

We stayed in Yang Shuo, a lushly, tropical jungle with rounded rock croppings jutting straight up out of the ground. A fog would roll in each afternoon as it rained, casting a pre-historic haze over the landscape.

We found a sweet Chinese girl to be our interpreter, and she got us settled into our hotel. Besides the thick wool blankets, there was netting around our beds and big bugs were smashed all over the walls. I had no idea bugs could be so big! Thank goodness we had netting. Once we were settled, she asked us if we would like to see a secret cave.

"Yes," I said instantly. Vickie and Elana weren't as enthusiastic, but went along with it.

We followed the girl into the jungle and down a trail that wound through banana trees. Birds were everywhere and their voices formed a choir. Nervously, the girl looked back over her shoulder and then ducked behind a banana tree. We ducked in behind her to see a deep hole in the ground. A rope dangled down into the darkness. She explained it was illegal for anyone to go into the cave, especially foreigners, but promised that no one would know. I was nervous but enticed.

She told us that, during the Japanese occupation, the entire town of Yangshuo hid in this cave for over a year. She said there was a fresh pool of water inside and the men left the cave at night to find food. The villagers were never discovered by the Japanese.

Elana and Vickie wanted to go back but I wanted to go down into the cave. "How often do you get to see something like this?" I said. Begrudgingly, they followed.

The girl asked us to take off our shoes and gave us flip-flops to wear. It seemed an odd trade-off for a climb, but I complied. Suddenly someone came in from behind the banana tree. We all jumped. I was ready to run.

"It's okay," said our interpreter. "She's here to help us."

The girls instructed us to climb down the side of the hole as we held on to the rope. The cave floor was twenty feet below us. I figured it must not be as bad as it looked or they wouldn't take us down there, especially in flip-flops. The girl's friend went in first, holding a flashlight at the bottom. I went in next.

The steep walls of the cave went straight up and down, and all I had to hang onto was the rope. I could see the small light below me. Shiny slick marks scuffed the walls where people had tried to use their feet. I clawed with my toes to slow myself down, trying to keep my flip-flops on. I wondered how we were going to get out.

Relieved, I finally felt the floor of the cave under my feet. I turned on my flashlight and glanced around the cave. It was enormous, with multiple chambers pointing in several different directions. I walked over to the perfectly clear, still water. There were pottery, plates, jugs, and other objects that the townspeople had used years earlier when they lived down there. I felt like I was stepping back through time.

The trip back up the rope was grueling. There were no footholds and the flip-flops kept us from getting traction on the walls. But eventually we made it, and the exhaustion and risk were worth the experience.

The next morning, we hiked Moon Mountain, also known as Immortal Mountain. Moon Mountain is a hill that has a natural arch running through it. Its large semi-circular hole can look like the stages of the moon when viewed from various angles. Again, the heat was stifling and our bodies were dripping wet.

I purposely hiked ahead of Vickie and Elana. I wanted space to think. Being in China had shown me how much I missed having a spiritual life. I continued to feel unworthy of God's love and I was troubled by it. What else could there be for me?

I finished the hike before Vickie and Elana and walked over to a clearing at the base of the trail. As I waited for them, I came upon an old Chinese man dressed in traditional robes. He appeared to be in his nineties. He was sitting on a log smoking a traditional long pipe. He motioned for me to come over and sit by him. I walked over, smiling. He smiled back, not a single tooth in his mouth.

I felt I was in the presence of a Chinese master. He smiled as he pulled a small box with rolling papers out of his robe. He sprinkled home-grown tobacco into it, licked it, and rolled it into a cigarette. He lit it and handed it to me. I had never been a smoker, but I wanted to see where this encounter would lead, especially in light of my thoughts that day. Who knew what wisdom these tendrils of smoke might impart to me?

I thanked him and inhaled. I coughed and choked as he burst into laughter, motioning with his hand for me to keep smoking. I stayed with it. I sat and looked at him, hoping to soak in any knowledge or wisdom he had to share. It was a poignant moment. I felt the heavens had opened and given me a message that there was a spiritual path for me and it was time for me to find it.

Vickie and Elana came into the clearing. He nodded his head to them, smiling. Feebly, he stood and slowly walked away.

Chapter 30
I Begin to Find My Way

I returned to Portland and ended a half-hearted relationship, deciding to be single while I figured myself out.

In January, I opened a medical clinic with Vickie and joined a meditation group committed to daily practice. At my first weekend meditation, Leong, our Buddhist meditation teacher, invited me to come up and sit in front of him. He was an older Asian man with a twinkle in his eye, not unlike the old Chinese man I had met in the clearing.

"You need to learn to be still," he said. "Instead of focusing on your breath as you meditate, focus only on what you feel."

As a woman who used running and extreme exercise to block out any feelings, this was a foreign idea, one I found nearly impossible. Sitting in quiet brought my emotions to the forefront, making me feel worse. Others in our group reported feeling peace and tranquility through their meditations. I just felt pain and misery.

I made a promise to stick with meditation, believing it would eventually bring me to the place of peace I craved and others were experiencing. It was tedious and painful. Waves of grief drowned me in sorrow. I would care for my patients at the clinic during the day and swim in darkness with my feelings at night.

My pleasure in simple things, like the smell of autumn leaves, taking a long walk in the park, or even climbing a mountain, faded. I wasn't sleeping well, and after six months I still could not sit peacefully while meditating. In fact, my body would jerk as I tried to keep it in one place. I wondered if I was capable of quiet meditation, yet I continued. I believed the only way I would break free of my despair was to feel every feeling I had worked so hard to bury.

Evenings became a ritual. Eat a tasteless dinner, light a candle and sit, maybe put on some music, and spend hours putting my emotions to paper as old memories returned.

At month six, I went to another weekend workshop. Leong took one look at me and could tell I had not reached meditation bliss. This time he asked me to meditate while sitting in front of him. He placed his finger lightly on my forehead, feeling the energy within me. He tapped me on the shoulder and asked me to open my eyes. He asked for the attention of the group and told us this story:

"There was a great teacher who traveled throughout China visiting different monasteries to work with the monks. One day he went to a monastery where the monks spent most of their days in silent meditation. He noticed that they were weak and sickly. Upon questioning, he learned they were eating healthy food, but had no physical movement in their daily routine. All of their time was spent in silent prayer and meditation, seeking enlightenment.

"The teacher rebuked the monks, explaining that they had missed one of the most important teachings, that the Qi, or energy of the body, must move in order to have both health and enlightenment. He then taught the monks how to do guided movements and asked them to practice this every day."

Leong then showed us an example of guided movements. He bowed to the four directions and went deeply inside himself. Slowly, he began to move in a way that looked similar to martial arts but with more emotion and incredible strength. His movements became stronger and faster. He explained to us that sometimes, in order for the body to relax, the static energy stuck within us must move. He explained that this energy was often associated with emotions, such as anger, grief, and even joy. He explained that after doing this exercise, it would be much easier to sit in silence.

The idea of moving resonated with me, and I was happy to try it that night at home. I bowed to the four directions and went inside myself to see what feelings were there and where I felt them in my body. I began to move. Slow movements became faster, anger in my gut started to move into my arms and legs. The more I moved, the angrier I became. Energy pulsed through my taut muscles as I moved ferociously about the room.

Twenty minutes passed quickly and I could feel fatigue setting in. Quick, hard movements became softer, as my body began to relax. And then sorrow hit. Profound grief emanated throughout my entire being, and I sank to the floor. Finally, I had reached that deepest place within me that I had worked so long to bury and protect. Tears ran down my cheeks and my heart ached. When the tears stopped, I took a breath deep into my belly, and for the first time since practicing meditation, I was able to sit peacefully.

Guided movements became a part of my evening ritual, the pathway to my feelings. Since it was easier now to sit still, I was able to focus on the emotions that surfaced. Painful memories would take me over, sometimes making me gag and vomit. It was as if all the feelings I had run from for years had united for a massive assault. They knocked me into a dark depression, the darkest I had ever known. I wondered if I was falling into a hole with no rope.

The darkness lasted a year before any light broke through. Then one minute of peace became two. Two became three. Within several months I enjoyed short periods of time without feeling tormented.

The darkness gradually lifted and the light woke me up. I used running and exercise less and less often to get away from my feelings and chose instead to sit with them, get them out and let them go.

I cannot find the words to describe the difference. Something inside of me began to change. My family, the Mormon Church, the many friends who had cut me out of their lives, none of that had changed. But somehow experiencing all of the feelings so deeply hidden within me had set me free.

The colors of the earth became brighter, a bird's song more beautiful, the sun was warmer, and life began to have meaning. Peace became my new reality rather than an elusive dream.

My thirst to find my own spiritual path was realized through meditation. I could be both a lesbian and spiritual. My friend, Lisa Good, sent this quote to me by the 14th Dalai Lama of Tibet which truly speaks to my beliefs: "My true religion is kindness."

I felt I had won my spiritual freedom. It was a victory that would give me strength for a battle I did not know was coming.

Chapter 31
Bishop at the Door

It was the summer of 1999. Life was good. Our clinic was doing well, I had a circle of wonderful friends, and I loved exploring the beautiful Pacific Northwest. My family and I had found a way to be together and avoid any discussion about me being a lesbian.

On a sunny day in the middle of July, a man came to my door, smiled, and identified himself as the Elder's Quorum President of the Mormon Church. Hearing he was from the church, I opened the screen door to talk to him.

"Hi, I am looking for Marnie Freeman," he said.

"I'm Marnie," I said.

"Okay, nice to meet you, Marnie," he said. "I'm here to see if you are interested in attending church."

"No, not at this time," I said.

"Well then, I would like to suggest you have home teachers," he said.

In the Mormon Church, home teachers come to your house each month to check on how you are doing and to give you a spiritual lesson.

"No, thanks," I said, smiling. "I really don't want home teachers at this time."

"Well, since you are not interested in attending church or having home teachers, have you considered taking your name off the records of the church?"

"No," I said, "I don't want my name removed."

"It is affecting the home teaching percentages we report to Salt Lake City," he said.

In the 35 years I had been in the church, I had never heard of anyone being asked to remove their name from the records because of attendance percentages.

"I'm sorry if it throws off your percentages," I said, "but I definitely do not want my name removed from the records of the church."

With that, he thanked me for my time and said goodbye. I closed the door and put the visit out of my mind.

Two weeks later, another man knocked on my door. This one was not smiling. In fact, I wondered if he had come to complain about my German Shepherd, Quincy, who got into mischief now and then.

"I'm looking for Marnie Freeman," he said. His tone was flat and serious.

"Yes?" I said.

"I'm looking for Marnie Freeman," he said again.

"Yes?" I repeated.

"Are you Marnie Freeman?" he asked.

"Yes, I am," I said.

"I am Bishop Weidler from the Mormon Church," he said.

Surprised, I smiled at him and opened the screen door. Bishops don't make house calls on inactive members. In fact, it is as likely that a Bishop comes to the home of an inactive member as it might be for a mayor to come to the home of a delinquent taxpayer, especially in a big city like Portland. It isn't done, as they don't have time to track down inactive members, of which there are untold numbers. Their hands are already more than full, taking care of their active congregations and all the problems and challenges that go with it.

Not only that, but Bishops are not paid, so they must carry out their responsibilities while also working. It is a consuming load to carry. I know this firsthand because my father and many of my male relatives have been, or are, Bishops or in the Bishopric.

So what would bring a Bishop to my door?

"Nice to meet you," I said. "What can I do for you?"

"I am here to urge you to have your name removed from the church membership if you are not active or interested in home teachers," he said.

I recalled the visit from the Elder two weeks earlier and guessed the Bishop's visit was a result of that visit, although I couldn't imagine how they found me since I had moved seven times since living in Salt Lake City. And it had been more than ten years since I had gone to church, and I had not requested to have my records transferred.

"Well, I am not interested in the church at this time, but I don't want my name removed from the church records," I said.

As a Mormon, when your name is removed from the church records it is removed from your family for eternity, as if someone stepped up to your family tree and erased your name. Being together here and in the afterlife is a sacred promise Mormon families live by. My parents would be heartbroken if my name was erased, and so would I. I loved my family and I wanted to remain a part of them, if not in religious practice, then by church record.

The Bishop was not pleased with my answer. He continued to insist I remove my name, and I continued to resist. In the back of my mind, I was watching the scene unfold as some sort of surreal drama that made no sense. Bishops don't do this.

He explained that my nonattendance was impacting the statistics he reported to church headquarters in Salt Lake City. He said he took his job very seriously and he was not going to have subpar statistics.

"If you are not going to attend church, or allow monthly home teachers, you should have your name removed from the records of the church," he repeated.

Again, I explained I did not want my name removed.

He pushed harder, unwilling to accept my answer.

When I realized he was not going to take no for an answer, or leave, I said, "Look, I am a lesbian. I have no desire to be involved with the church, but I do not want my name removed from the records at this time."

The Bishop leaned toward me, close enough for me to smell his breath. "You are a lesbian?"

"Yes," I said, looking straight into his eyes.

He raised his voice. "Do you realize you are not living within accordance of the standards of the church and it is my job to hold a church court?"

"No other Bishop in my life has ever said that," I answered.

"As a Bishop, it is my responsibility to be a judge in Israel. I would not want to meet my Maker without living up to that responsibility," he said. "To be a member of the church you must repent and come back to the church. And if you still have those feelings, you cannot act on them."

"I guess you are going to have to do what you feel you must do," I said. "I do not believe you have the right to judge me. You don't even know who I am."

"You are wrong. The Bishops and Stake Presidents are given the right to judge. It is my job to be a judge in Israel."

Keeping my voice steady, I said, "You have no idea what it is to live my life. Until you have walked in my shoes, you have no right to judge me."

"We all make judgments, even you," he said. "I have nine kids and I judge them all the time." The fact that he used the word "judge" rather than "teach" his kids revealed the depth of his belief in judgment.

"I do not feel I have the right to judge any person," I said. "There is no way we as individuals can understand another person's pain, or what they have been through in their lives."

"Well, you must not know the scriptures," he said, "and I follow the scriptures literally." He had turned hostile. He had come to enforce and I was an unflinching resistor.

"You are a man, and what you are saying now is coming from a man," I said. "Christ would not stand at my door and say these things to me, especially in this way. The church is about love and kindness, not judgment and punishment. This is not the spirit of the law. It might be the letter of the law, but it is not the spirit of the law."

"I follow the letter of the law. That is my job," he said.

"It is a sad thing," I said, "but there is no place in the Mormon Church for people like me."

He responded, "The church has been this way for a long time, and I don't see it changing anytime soon. Other people have come to me about same sex relationships and the same thing has happened to them."

"It is odd to me that all of the Bishops in my life, except one, have treated me with love and kindness," I said. "My father is in the Stake Presidency in Utah and he would never stand at someone's door and treat him or her this way. He goes out of his way to treat people with respect."

My words took him by surprise. "Your father is in the Stake Presidency?" Stake Presidents are over Bishops.

"Yes," I said.

My words seemed to fire him up even more. He would set my father and my previous Bishops straight. Indignantly, he said,

"I would be happy to call your father and any of your past Bishops." He added, "It is also my responsibility to inform the Stake President here in Portland and notify the High Councilmen."

I was familiar with the church's chain of command and figured he would talk with the Stake President, but I knew that talking with the High Councilmen over something like this was extremely unusual. Bishop Weidler was now on a righteous hunt and it appeared that I was his next prey.

"You do not know me. You do not know my life," I said. "I am a kind, honest person. I cannot believe I will be cast into hell because of what I feel in my heart."

He stepped closer, almost into my living room. I took a step back while keeping my eyes on him. Angrily, he said, "It is my job to hold a church court. I'm sure you probably have a problem with the fact that this council will be made up of all men?"

He was baiting me. I didn't bite. I was in that zone of absolute focus and calm; there was not any way that I was going to get angry. Thinking for a moment, I said, "Yes, as a matter of fact I do have a problem with that. I think it would be much fairer if I were to be judged by my peers, possibly six men and six women. Or, since I am a woman, perhaps I should be judged by all women."

"The church is a patriarchal organization," he hissed. "That is why the men hold the priesthood. Women are equal, but the men hold the priesthood, as well as the governing positions in the church. Ruth never held the priesthood; Esther never held the priesthood."

"I do think it is too bad that the women of the church cannot hold the priesthood," I said. "And yes, I do feel they would be every bit as capable of running the church as men." I added, "My relatives were the original Utah pioneer settlers who traveled across the plains with Brigham Young. I come from a long line of strong women of the church."

"How many of them were lesbian?" he asked.

I let his words hang in the air, then said, "You have to do what you have to do. But know this, one day you will look back on this day with regret. You will realize that no person has the right to treat another with disrespect and unkindness. You will realize that Christ is about Love and Kindness. You will realize that it would have been better to have walked away from my door. How is leaving my name on the records of the church hurting anyone in any way?"

With that, he said, "I am going to start church proceedings against you." He turned and walked away. Choosing to hold an official church court depends on the facts of the situation and is generally left to the discretion of the Bishop or Stake President.

Trembling, I closed the door. I leaned back against it and slid to the floor, placing my forehead on my knees. It was very possible that I was going to be tried for being who I was, for being a lesbian.

Like most Mormons, I was terrified of having a church court. It was the mysterious, awful place you never wanted to be. If Bishop Weidler had his way, I would appear in his court for him to personally ex-communicate me. The outcome would improve his percentages and strengthen his obedience to the letter of the law.

I went upstairs and cried. It wasn't the cry of a frightened girl, it was the cry of a woman judged unfit by men in the name of God, a woman whose faith was rooted in kindness and who believed in respect for all.

Chapter 32
I'm Called to Court

It would not be easy, but I would come through whatever was ahead. My name would not be erased from my family without them hearing my story and understanding who I was. I would need to be strong. When my tears cleared, I wrote and dated everything Bishop Weidler and I had spoken to one another.

The following Sunday, I told my sister Jana about the Bishop's house call and his intention to hold a Church Court. She knew Bishops didn't make visits like that, and certainly not with a hostile attitude, and she urged me to tell my father.

I agreed with her, and at the same time I didn't want to have another difficult conversation with Dad related to my sexuality. We had reached a place of peace because we didn't talk about it anymore. Jana was right, though; I needed Dad's help.

I called Dad and told him the story. He felt the Bishop was out of line and asked me to document the details in an email to him, which I did that night. By the next day, Dad had spoken to the Stake President in Portland. I felt loved and supported to have my father defend me even though he did not approve of my lifestyle. He would not condone someone treating me unfairly, even a Mormon Bishop.

Within minutes of speaking with my father, the Portland Stake President, Mike Laboe, called me. We talked for about forty-five minutes. He seemed to be a kind man. He was curious about how Bishop Weidler came to my door, saying, "Bishops do not go to the doors of inactive members. How did this come about?" I explained that someone had come two weeks before, and the Bishop two weeks later.

He said, "And you have never met or had interaction with this Bishop?"

"No," I said. He seemed baffled.

He apologized for the way the Bishop had conveyed his message and emphasized that church courts are courts of love, not punishment or discipline. "They are a way to lead those who have strayed back to the flock," he said.

He told me Bishop Weidler had already begun official court proceedings against me. He explained my father had asked him to take over jurisdiction because Bishop Weidler had been so disrespectful. Dad felt the Bishop could not objectively govern my court.

President Laboe was hesitant to take jurisdiction because he said it had not been done before, and because he wanted to give the Bishop every opportunity to redeem himself, to learn something from this experience.

President Laboe asked me to call Bishop Weidler to express my concerns. He wanted me to share them with the Bishop, including my concern about his ability to be objective. Then, depending upon the Bishop's response, I could make one of the following choices:

1. Bishop Weidler would preside over my court.

2. Bishop Weidler would preside over my court and President Laboe would also be in attendance.

3. President Laboe would take jurisdiction and there would be a high council court.

In other words, my choice would be to appear in Bishop Weidler's court with him as my judge and jury or to choose the higher court made up of many men I did not know.

A Bishop's Court, otherwise known as a Disciplinary Council, is convened by the Bishop of a ward - in this case, Bishop

Weidler. The council is composed of the Bishop, his two counselors and the ward clerk. The Bishop's Court is for cases against men who hold the lower priesthood and for the women of the church. After hearing the evidence of the case, a vote is taken to determine the membership of the accused.

Church courts can result in disciplinary action, such as probation, dis-fellowship, and in some cases ex-communication. A vote is taken, but the Bishop has the power to veto.

A High Council Court, on the other hand, is convened by the Stake President when a member of the highest priesthood - the Melchizedek priesthood - has committed a serious offense that may result in ex-communication. The High Council Court consists of the Stake President, his two Counselors, the twelve members of the Stake High Council, and a Clerk to take notes of the proceedings. Lots are drawn, and six of the High Council Members advocate for the accused, and six take a position against the accused during the trial and in the process of questioning. In the end, a vote is taken to determine the outcome. Like the Bishop, the Stake President can overrule the votes.

For members that are placed on probation or dis-fellowshipped, their offense is removed permanently from their record once they have repented and the conditions of being dis-fellowshipped have been met. In the case of ex-communication, the ex-communicated person is permanently removed from the records of the church. There are certain offenses that follow you; in other words, they will always be on your church record, and you will never be free of their stigma and consequence. They include things like murder, adultery, incest, spousal abuse, and homosexuality.

Because I did not currently hold a position of leadership in the church and had not ever gone through the temple to receive my endowments, I hoped it was possible that I could be dis-fellowshipped as opposed to ex-communicated.

"Bishop Weidler is one of my better Bishops," he said. "I think he can really do this. You just caught him on a bad day."

As much as I didn't want to, I agreed to make the call. I dreaded calling the Bishop. I never wanted to speak to the man again, and I didn't feel he deserved a second chance. I knew it was unlikely there was anything I could do to change his mind or his judgments. Plus, I struggled with the fact that I was asked to call him, rather than the other way around. If President Laboe wanted the Bishop to learn from this experience, shouldn't he be the one calling me?

Still, I liked President Laboe enough to give the Bishop a second chance.

A week-and-a-half later, I called the Bishop and left a message at his home. He didn't call back.

I waited a week then called him at the church. He picked up the phone.

"Hello," I said. "This is Marnie Freeman. President Laboe asked me to call you to talk about what happened between us at my house in July, to share my concerns with you."

He said, "Yes?"

I waited for him to lead the conversation; instead, he said nothing. So I explained what had made me uncomfortable about the encounter.

"First, you didn't identify yourself at the door," I said. "As a woman, this is a red flag."

"I wasn't sure if the door would be slammed in my face," he said.

"I was offended at the comment you made about my relatives," I said.

"I don't remember saying anything about that," he said. "A person can't remember every single thing they say during a conversation."

I felt bolder as I went along. I said I was offended by the aggressive way he dealt with me, that it seemed he was baiting me with the comment about my having a problem with there being only men on my jury. I told him I didn't feel that he acted with kindness and love, which is the entire point of the church. I said I felt he might be homophobic and biased, and because of that I did not feel comfortable with him leading my court.

He remained silent.

I waited until it was clear he was not going to speak, and then I said, "Do you honestly feel you came to my door with love and kindness?"

After a long pause, he said, "I look back and I may not have had the Spirit of the Lord with me that day."

He continued, "I held a court on another lesbian and it went poorly. I may have assumed my interaction with you would be like my interaction with her."

The conversation ended stiffly. I began to realize being dis-fellowshipped was a far-reaching hope; ex-communication was much more likely.

The next day I received a letter from Bishop Weidler dated August 4, just four days after he came to my door. For some reason that I don't know, he had waited to send it.

> *Dear Sister Marnie Freeman:*
>
> *The Bishopric of the Alameda Ward of the Portland Oregon East Stake is considering formal disciplinary action against you. This may include the possibility of dis-fellowshipment or ex-communication because you are reported to have been guilty of moral conduct unbecoming a member of the Church.*
>
> *You are invited to attend this disciplinary council to give your response and, if you wish, to provide witnesses to other evidence in your behalf.*
>
> *This disciplinary council will be held Wednesday, September 22, 1999, starting at 8:00 P.M. in the Alameda ward Bishop's office. Should you wish to discuss this with me prior to the council date please call me.*

Sincerely,

Bishop Donald Weidler

I took a week to think about my choices and talk them over with my sister Jana, my parents, and my Aunt Mary Anne, all active Mormons. They agreed they would not want to be judged by this Bishop.

I called the Stake President. If he and the Bishop had talked about the call, he wasn't letting on.

"How'd it go?" he asked. "Do you feel better after talking to the Bishop?"

"No, not at all," I said.

"I feel strongly that the Bishop should reside over your court," he said. "I will attend in support of you, but the Bishop is the one to do the court."

"But you told me I had the choice of courts," I said.

"This is really the Bishop's right and jurisdiction, Marnie," he said.

I read the Bishop's letter to him and asked if he thought it was fair for me to be considered guilty before being tried. I reminded him that he had told me the purpose of court was to lovingly guide someone back, not to discipline them.

"You said it was my choice," I said. "Now you're saying I have no choice."

"I don't remember giving you that choice," he said.

"I wrote down exactly what you said in our last conversation," I said. "You asked me to call the Bishop to give him a second chance and that if I still felt uncomfortable having him lead my court, you would preside."

President Laboe encouraged me to stay with the Bishop's Court. He said the Higher Court would be a circus. He felt the outcome of the two courts would be the same, so for me to go through the pain of being judged by so many men seemed unnecessary to him.

I told him I preferred the High Court over the Bishop's Court.

With a deep sigh, he said, "All right. I do not want to add to the injustice you have already experienced. I will preside and your case will be moved to the High Court."

As horrible as it sounded to sit in front of all of these men I did not know, I was relieved not to have Bishop Weidler as my judge.

We agreed on a court date of September 28, 1999 at 8:30 P.M., six weeks away. President Laboe and I would speak again a week before the actual court date.

My family was relieved by the decision. We discussed the issues around the case but never the actual issue itself. At the end of August, I went to Salt Lake for a family reunion Jana had planned long before the Bishop came to my door. It was a heartwarming relief from the nagging worry about the pending court appearance. As difficult as it was, I felt supported by my family.

No one said it, but we were all aware that this could be the last time I would be with them as a Mormon-recognized member of the family.

I had always been Mormon, and it was sad to me that I wouldn't be one for very much longer.

Chapter 33
I Prepare for Court

The month leading up to my appearance in Church Court was an emotional one. On the one hand, I was depressed. I had every reason to believe I would be ex-communicated from my church and that my name would be blotted out from my family tree in the church records. And even though I hadn't attended church for twelve years, I was about to officially lose touch with a community of people I loved and that I had been a part of all of my life.

On the other hand, I was inspired. I would have an opportunity to speak honestly before seventeen leaders - judges - of the church, particularly the Stake President and the 12 men in the high council. I did not hold the hope that I would change their minds, but maybe my words would cause just one of them to soften his approach regarding this issue. It would not help me, but it might help someone in the future.

I began to think about mounting a defense on my behalf. I wouldn't disagree with my alleged crime - indeed, I was a lesbian. Instead, I would show these men that I was a *normal* human being, that I had hopes and dreams, heartaches and disappointments, just like all of them. I would show that I was a loving, kind, respectful person, and that I believed there was a place for everyone in God's Kingdom.

My hope was that if they could see who I truly was, that I was no different than their wives or daughters, perhaps they could soften how they perceived people like me. I knew I had no hope of changing the outcome of my court.

I Prepare for Court

I thought ahead as to what kind of support I would need on the day of court. I asked some of my best friends to be there to support me. They were people who loved me no matter what and who truly knew my heart and who I was in the world.

I decided against inviting anyone in my family because I knew, if they were there, I would be worrying about how they felt, and it would be harder for me to keep my focus.

Late one evening, I called Grams to ask if she would write a letter to the court on my behalf. "Absolutely," she said. "I would be proud to write a letter for you." My parents each agreed to write letters, too.

My defense was set.

As planned, President Laboe and I spoke a week before my court date. Again, he implored me to have a regular Bishop's court, with far fewer men there.

"Marnie, there could be as many as 19 men there," he said.

I said, "No, I am not comfortable having Bishop Weidler lead my court."

He paused, then said, "Bishop Weidler would like to be there. Would you mind?"

My throat tightened. Bishop Weidler was the last person on earth I would want at my court. The obedient Mormon, who was still inside of me somewhere, wanted to give his wishes more importance than my own and say, *Sure, he can be there.* However, the woman I had become knew court would be difficult enough for me without having Bishop Weidler there.

"I'm sorry," I said. "I don't want him to be at my court."

I slept very little the night before court. In a few hours, I would be in a room alone with 19 men judging me on my sexuality. The thought made me want to vomit.

I woke before dawn, put on my meditation beads, and sleepily made my way over to sit in front of my altar. It was going to take everything I had to get through this day. The phone rang a couple of times, but I did not answer. I felt weak and needed to protect myself from any well-meaning conversations.

I wasn't sure who would be calling, because I'd told my family I would not talk with any of them that day. I knew I could not bear to hear their heartbreak, especially on a day when my own was so raw. I told them I would call when I was ready. Dad understood, but Mom said, "Of course you won't let too much time go by." I appreciated their support but stood firm and repeated that I would call when I was ready.

At about ten o'clock that morning, I went downstairs to listen to my voice mail messages. I was surprised and pleased to discover that all of my family had respected my wishes. There were no last-minute pleas to change my mind. Surprisingly, my Aunt MaryAnn had called and asked me to call her back.

Aunt MaryAnn had been an important support in my life since the day she picked me up after I'd been expelled from BYU. I knew she loved me. I had adored her as my favorite aunt since I was a little girl. I used to set the table at dinner at my grandmother's house and I'd be sure to sit next to Aunt MaryAnn. I always gave us matching purple cups.

I trusted Aunt MaryAnn and decided to make an exception and call her back. I was in dire need of her love and support.

My hand shook as I dialed her number, and she quickly picked up the phone.

"How are you doing?" she asked.

"I'm feeling really sad," I said, "but I'm feeling strong and confident in my decision."

Aunt MaryAnn said, "Marnie, I need to tell you something. I need to be honest with you. I know you are doing the wrong thing. Being a lesbian is wrong, and it will never be accepted by the church. This will never bring you happiness."

Her words took me by surprise and I began to cry.

She continued. "Marnie I have never told you how I honestly feel. Wouldn't you prefer my honesty?"

Between sobs, I said, "Yes, but not today." I told her I loved her and I appreciated that she could finally be honest with me, but today was not the day to do it.

I explained to her that it was going to take everything I had to get through my court that night. I was not strong enough to hear these words from her. I said that I had mistaken her silence as support, or at least understanding.

As my tears splashed on the counter in front of me, I said, "I have to go. Goodbye."

I had to pull myself back together. The day was slipping by quickly.

I didn't feel like eating, so I decided to fast for the day, using anything positive to get me ready for the inquisition that lay ahead. I spent the day journaling, meditating, and praying for strength and wisdom. Even though I had thought through the words I would say to the court many times, I still wasn't settled on what I would say. Hours before court, I prayed to God to give me the words that would most impact the men I would stand before, words that would touch their hearts and soften the way they looked at people like me.

Chapter 34
Court Convenes

At 6:30 PM. I showered and got dressed. Vicki and Tina arrived at my house half an hour later. My court would begin at 8:00.

President Laboe asked me to arrive thirty minutes early so we could meet face to face for the first time and talk before court convened.

Fear coursed through me as we drove to the Stake House. It was a dark, moonless night. As instructed, I drove around to the back of the building where a light was on. I got out of the car, opened the familiar glass doors that open to all Mormon Stake Houses, and focused on putting one foot in front of the other. Nausea coursed through me. My chest felt tight as I gulped air. Vicki and Tina were quiet.

The Stake House holds the offices of the Stake president, his counselors, and the High Council. These are the people that oversee the Bishops and their congregations, or wards. A church is typically made up of two or three wards. However, four to six wards meet at a Stake House for special meetings and conferences.

Even though I had never physically been in this particular Stake House, the familiarity of the building was overwhelming. I walked down the carpeted halls that looked the same as every Stake House I had ever entered, and passed the bathrooms, which were placed where all others were. I knew the Stake President's office would be in the very center of the building and found it easily. I stopped when I saw the light coming from President Laboe's half open door. Vicki and Tina looked at me reassuringly as I stepped forward to knock. The door swung slowly open as I peered inside.

A distinguished, slightly balding, fifty-something man looked up. President Laboe stood and shook my hand, motioning for me to sit down. Instead of sitting behind his desk, he sat in a chair close to mine, which I interpreted as a gesture of respect and kindness.

He introduced himself, and then jokingly said, "Well, you don't look any different than anyone else. You're attractive and obviously bright."

I couldn't help but wonder what he was expecting. Even though there didn't seem to be malice behind his words, he clearly did not feel I was the same as everyone else. I decided his comment came from his discomfort at what I knew must be a difficult situation for him to be in, as well as for me.

"Do you have any questions," he asked.

"No," I said.

He explained the process. My friends and I would wait in a holding room, just outside his office. He and the High Councilmen would meet first. They would begin with prayer, and then he would announce that they were going to have a court tonight. He had not told them prior to the meeting because he did not want to risk an information leak or pre-conceived notions. He would read my father's letter before ushering me into the room.

"Why did you choose my father's letter over the letter written by my mother?"

"I felt your father's letter was less emotional and gave more of your history," he said.

I looked in his eyes and asked, "If this were your church court, is my father's letter the one you would read to represent yourself?" I asked this to find out if his choice was for patriarchal reasons rather than for effectiveness.

"Yes it is," he said. Then, with gentleness in his eyes, he added, "Marnie, are you currently in a relationship?"

"No," I said.

"Technically, then, you are not living a lesbian lifestyle," he said, "which means you are not living outside the confines of the church."

Politely, I interrupted him before he went further. "I am a lesbian, and it will only be a matter of time before I am in a relationship," I said. "If the intention of the church is to hold courts for gay and lesbian members, then we should move forward. I would much rather do it now, than have to do it again later."

Resigned, he leaned back in his chair and continued to explain how court would unfold.

The first part of the court would be the trial portion and I would be in there alone. My friends could join me during my defense. I asked if they could be with me the entire time, but he said that people in the past have gotten too emotional, so they would need to stay in the holding area.

The High Council would draw straws. Six men would prosecute me and six men would defend me, which simply meant they would speak up if something unfair occurred. Two of the six prosecutors would conduct all of the questioning. When the two were finished, the remaining councilmen could ask questions they felt were unanswered.

"Do you understand the process," he asked.

"Basically, yes," I said. "But I will understand more when it actually happens."

He asked if I had any other questions, and when I didn't, he asked me to return to the holding area.

The holding area was a narrow, oblong room with four chairs lined up side by side. At the end of the room was a large, dark door. Beyond the door was the trial room. I swallowed what felt like cotton in my throat, staying as far from the door as I could. Vicki and Tina were seated in two of the chairs and two other friends, Ruth and Sara, arrived just as I walked in from talking with President Laboe.

I paced. Every nerve in my body jittered.

As kids we'd heard rumors about this room. None of us had actually seen it, but we knew it was where serious meetings and ex-communications happened. I recalled times we stood outside the big doors, wondering in whispers what really went on behind them. I would soon find out.

I heard the muffled sounds of the High Councilmen entering the room from a separate entrance. I started to sweat, and combined with my nausea, it was all I could do to keep pacing. I could hear their voices, but could not understand their words. As my fear mounted, tears stung my eyes. I turned away from my friends. I bit my lip, I bit my cheek, I did everything I could to choke my feelings down. I was not going to walk into that room crying.

Sara saw me struggling, and asked me if I wanted a hug. I turned toward her and saw that all of my friends had tears in their eyes, too. I looked away quickly, saying, "Don't look at me and don't touch me." I knew any act of kindness would be my undoing. They understood. All of us were teetering on the edge.

What felt like an hour was only twenty minutes. We heard the click of a door handle as the big door slowly swung open.

President Laboe stepped into the room, closed the door behind him, and said, "Marnie, please don't do this. Don't make me put you through this. Leave now and let us hold the court without you."

I held back my tears and said, "No, I need to see this through. The men in that room need to hear what I have to say."

"But Marnie," he said, "you won't change any of their minds."

"If I come away from this with one person in that council room looking at this issue differently," I said, "it will have been worth it. You are the men that govern the church here, and there are young kids out there just like me."

"Okay," he said. "Do you need another minute?"

"No," I said. I took a gulp of air that felt like jagged cement sliding down my throat, and I stepped through the door.

He turned to my friends and said he would be back for them in about thirty minutes, not realizing it would be an hour-and-a-half.

President Laboe opened the door and motioned me ahead of him. My first sense of the room was the stale air. The room had no windows because it was in the center of the building. Then I saw the longest table I had ever seen. It was dark walnut. Around the table were big-armed, deep leather chairs, each filled with a man.

As I entered the room, the men stood, getting their first look at me.

President Laboe motioned for me to take the chair at the far end of the table. I felt their eyes follow me as I walked to my seat. How could such a short distance feel so long? When I reached my seat, they motioned for me to sit down, as they, too, sat down.

Right away, I zeroed in on a youngish man who had the same air about him as Bishop Weidler. I hoped he would not be one of my questioners. I turned my focus to President Laboe as he explained to me that he had read my father's letter before I came in, and that the designated councilmen were ready to begin their questioning. He pointed to the two men that would question me. Sure enough, the man I had hoped to avoid was one of my questioners. The second man, however, looked like the kindest man there.

"Before the questions begin," I said to President Laboe, "could each person around the table give me their name?"

"Yes, we can do that," he said.

It is common in the Mormon Church to call people by Brother or Sister and use their last name, for example, Brother Hansen. So I was impressed as all but one of the men spoke their first and last names.

Once all of the men had identified themselves, my questioning began. The assertive man jumped in first.

High Councilman 1 asked, "Do you take Jesus Christ to be your Savior?"

I answered, "I believe Christ was a great man and teacher. I also believe there have been other great people in this world. I think about Gandhi, the Dalai Lama, the Pope, Mother Teresa, and others. With the many religions in this world, it does not make sense to me that there is only one way to be saved."

High Councilman 1 asked, "Do you believe Christ died for your sins?"

I answered, "I believe all of us come into this world in a state of perfection. I believe we all make mistakes. I believe we must all suffer the consequences of our actions, whatever they may be. It is hard for me to fathom that my redemption is based on the suffering of another person. It seems to me that I will be judged by my actions, and what is in my heart. Nothing more. Nothing less."

High Councilman 1 asked, "Do you believe the Mormon Church to be the restored true church of God?"

I answered, "I believe there are many great religions in this world. Most of them do not take Christ as their Savior. How can one religion be better or truer than another?"

The questions continued and then High Councilman 2 asked a question.

"Currently, are you engaged in acts that are unbecoming of

Christ?"

I looked at him directly and respectfully and asked, "What do you mean?"

He said, "Are you currently practicing acts that would be unacceptable in the Mormon Church?"

I said, "I live my life as best I can. Sometimes I absolutely make mistakes. However, I feel I can say that, for the most part, I live the best life possible. I treat all people with kindness. I am accepting of people who are different than me. I am a health care practitioner. There will never be a day in my practice when someone is turned away because they can't pay. So my answer to you is this - I am not perfect, but I am living the best life I know how."

A third High Councilman, the youngest in the room, sounding impatient, interrupted with a question of his own. "Are you living within God's commandments? Is there not a commandment that states you must not commit adultery?"

I turned to High Councilman 3 and said, "By my definition, adultery would be a married person having sexual relations with someone other than their spouse. No I am not."

High Councilman 3 said, "Anyone having relations outside the bond of marriage is committing adultery."

I said, "Do I have the option to be married in the Mormon Church?"

"No," he said.

I said, "It seems unfair to me to be judged by a law I am not able to practice. Does that really seem fair to you? You are telling me I cannot do something, and then because I am not doing it, I am going to be judged by that law and punished."

High Councilman 3 responded, "You are living outside the confines of the standards of the church."

Looking at President Laboe I said, "May I ask a question?"

"Yes," he said.

"Does the Mormon Church uphold marriages performed outside of the Mormon Church?" I asked. "Are these people adulterers, or are they living within the law?"

In unison, the councilmen nodded their heads *yes*. Someone said, "We uphold all common law marriages outside of the church."

I turned to High Councilman 3 and said, "In the State of Vermont, gay and lesbian marriages are legal. If I were married in Vermont, would I still be sitting in this court? Since my union would be legal and binding, would it be recognized by the church?"

High Councilman 3 said, "That is not the point."

I looked over at President Laboe and saw him look away as he smiled. I nodded to him, indicating I was finished.

President Laboe asked the High Councilmen if there were any other questions and they shook their heads *No*. He looked at me and said, "I will bring in your friends."

As I watched each of my friends enter the room, I could see the impact of the sobering scene on them. Their eyes were moist as they walked to their seats. I was so relieved to see their loving faces, and my eyes connected with each of them as they sat down. Their presence gave me strength.

It was time for my defense.

My friend Ruth, a brilliant attorney, had wanted to stand and defend me. I was grateful for her offer, but I felt it best to represent myself. I wanted these men to hear my story in my own words and from my own mouth.

Chapter 35
My Defense

I opened my defense by reading the letter Grams wrote because she was the one person in the family to truly accept me the way I was. She had never said to me, "I love you but I don't agree with you." With Grams there were no "but's."

I read my eighty four-year-old grandmother's letter, the matriarch of our family:

September 15, 1999

As I write this about my cherished, sweet, Granddaughter, Marnie Freeman, I go deep into my heart and soul, which brings back so many wonderful, stirring, fond memories of a sweet little girl (most of the time) and the many beautiful and harmonious times we spent together as she grew up. My life is richer, better, and happier because of Marnie. My love for her is unconditional and I accept and love her the way she is. Thank you Marnie for the part you played in my life to bring me joy.

I have a testimony of the gospel of Jesus Christ. I love the Savior and am thankful for all he did for me.

My goal in this life is to develop the same love Christ has for all of us. It is a big task, but I am trying. To me the full purpose of the gospel is to help each one of us to become better. To learn to love others as we have been loved. It is not for recognition or glory, but in our hearts to develop tolerance, charity, understanding, kindness, patience and love. Being able to put ourselves in another's shoes. If the Gospel of Jesus Christ doesn't do that, in my opinion it has failed.

I have a hard time understanding people that proclaim they have a tes-

timony of the gospel and yet are so quick to judge others. For example, my older sister's son was sent to prison because of a crime he committed. His father died while he was in prison, his mother died of a broken heart. He was alone. I made many trips to the prison the seven years he was there.

Certainly, it was difficult for me to understand why he did what he did; however, it is not my place to judge. My job is to love him unconditionally as I would love my own children.

My three brothers, two of whom are stake presidents, and my three sisters, from that time forward, never recognized him as part of our family. No cards on his Birthday or Christmas, and no visits.

He is out of prison now and doing very well. Love is so important and saves lives.

We are always so quick to judge. If only it were possible to look deeply into one another's lives, to possibly walk in another's "shoes" for just one day. How differently we may treat them.

The purpose of the Gospel of Jesus Christ, I believe, is to further our ability to love others. I feel, the sad part is, too many in leadership positions in the church let and inject their own views and personality, which influences their judgment of others.

I love, support, and sustain each Prophet of our church. When President Benson became our prophet, he brought so much love, kindness, and tolerance; and many routine things were changed. I love and sustain President Hinckley. His father was my mission president. I know President Hinckley personally. His philosophy is to love all people. To love the members into activity into the church.

It is my opinion that the only thing that really matters in this life is the way that we treat others. Because I have not walked in Marnie's shoes, I cannot judge her. How can we judge anyone? I feel these matters must be left to the Lord.

But I know Marnie. I know her heart. I am proud she is my granddaughter. Even though we have a different life style, I love her and accept her as she is.

There are some things we just don't understand, and they need to be left to the Lord. If you could look into her life, you would be overwhelmed with her goodness.

Thanks again, Marnie. I love you.

Grams

Lucy Freeman McBride

I explained to the Councilmen that when my grandmother sent her letter, she also sent a small green box. Inside the box was a familiar ruby ring and necklace. Grams had worn that ring for the past 35 years. I slid the ring from my finger and held it up for them to see.

"My grandmother is the strongest woman I know," I said. "When she was pregnant with her sixth child, for reasons I will not say, she asked for a divorce from my grandfather, who was a Bishop. She was left homeless with three young children to raise on her own.

"The first Christmas after my grandparents' divorce, my grandmother was terribly sad and didn't have any money. She took her wedding ring to a pawnshop, got half its value back in cash, and bought a beautiful ruby ring, which is on my finger today. Divorce was rare in the Mormon Church at that time, so my grandmother's shame stopped her from telling us the story behind this ruby ring, which she wore most of her life. This week she not only told me the story of her ruby ring, but sent it to me with this enclosed note:

Dear Marnie:
I love you so much and stand by you. I always will. I had this ring ready to send you on your Birthday, but will send it early so you can wear it on September 28. Look at it that day and it will remind you I love you as a circle and will continue forever - No end. Love Grams.

"My Grandmother recently had her large intestine removed because it was filled with cancer. I don't know how long I will have her, but it will break my heart to lose the one person in my family that loves me as she does - unconditionally."

After reading my grandmother's note, I summarized my life for them. I told them I had felt different all of my life. I told them about my confessions to my Bishop in Monterey, that I had told him how I felt, and that I had never acted on it. I told them about the handout given to me entitled *To The One* and how, as a young girl of seventeen, it was heartbreaking to read. I told them about Bishop Roberts telling me that if I were to be hung on a cross, I would belong between a murderer and a pedophile. I told them how I had gone to my Bishop for help, only to come away feeling guilt-ridden and alone.

I told them about my experience at BYU, how I was ordered to sit in front of a man's desk for thirty minutes each day with him looking at me with contempt and disgust. I told them his last words to me, "If it were up to me you would never step foot on this campus, you would never step foot in Provo, and you would never be allowed back in to this state. We do not need people like you." I told them how this experience filled me with incredible guilt, humiliation, and shame.

I told them about riding the bus home after I had been expelled, stopping in San Francisco to change buses, and looking out over the city, wondering if I would ever find people like me. I explained that because of my Bishop's breach of confidentiality, my community never again accepted me. I was never invited to missionary farewells, best friend's weddings, receptions, or homes for that matter. I told them I couldn't sleep, and I walked the streets every night, in utter despair.

I told them I had moved to Utah a couple of years later to start over, that I had joined a young adult ward, and had confessed my feelings and my actions to the Bishop. I told them he had promised to find a solution for me and that for the first time in my life, I felt true hope that I could be "normal."

I told them he never called and wouldn't call me back when I called him, and how on that final night, when I realized my Bishop was never going to call, that there was no answer for me, that I went into my bedroom and raised a gun to my head, feeling totally hopeless.

I looked at each of them and said, "You are the leaders of this church. Do not think there are not many more people like me. I promise you there are. They might be too fearful to come forward with their feelings, but I guarantee they are there. When you think about the teenage suicide rate, particularly the youth dealing with this issue, you will realize how important every word is that you say. How even one small joke, or homophobic remark could make the difference between someone's life or their death. The people in this stake are looking to you for love, kindness, and understanding."

I paused for a moment and looked at each man. I said, "I hope each and every one of you always remembers this day. You profess to be the latter day church of Christ. If Christ were sitting at this table, I do not believe this would be happening. There is not any place in the Bible where Christ did anything like this. The one thing he said over and over was 'Let them come unto me...' Never did he ex-communicate them from him. Christ's love is about unconditional acceptance of all people."

President Laboe thanked me for my remarks and said my friends and I would need to wait in the holding room. As I stood, I felt a huge weight had been lifted from my shoulders. No longer was I fighting back my tears. A calm had come over me.

Chapter 36
The Verdict

We waited in the holding area about five minutes and were ushered back into the court room. President Laboe said, "We are left with no other option but to ex-communicate you from the church. You are living a life unbecoming of Christ."

He asked me to shake the hand of each of the Councilmen. I felt put on the spot and didn't want to shake their hands, especially after being told I was living a life unbecoming of Christ. But then I thought, "I can finish this." I did not want anything to detract from why I was really there.

I looked each man straight in the eye as I shook his hand. Without exception, each man said, "Thank you." However, only one man held my gaze. He said, "Thank you. I was touched by your thoughts tonight."

As I left the Stake House that cold, dark night, enormous warmth ran through me. It was the special warmth that comes from being true to yourself and being proud of it.

Later that week, President Laboe called me to see how I was doing. "Of your prosecutors, I think you ended up with one of the kindest men in the room and one of the toughest."

"I agree," I said.

"Why did you let High Councilman 3 off the hook when you had him cornered," he asked.

I thought for a moment and said, "I knew what I had to say would not change the outcome of the court in any way. High Councilman 3 was the youngest man there, and I didn't want to humiliate him in front of the older councilmen."

President Laboe said, "You know, Marnie you are okay. I am really sorry this had to happen. I think your parents would have been extremely proud of you the other night."

On September 30, I received a letter from one of the councilmen who was a member of my court. Perhaps it was the man who spoke to me at the end. He wrote:

> *Dear Sister Freeman:*
>
> *Thank you for the comments you gave the other evening at our High Council meeting. You touched my heart very deeply.*
>
> *You are a very impressive young woman. You were not overly aggressive, but you made your point; you were not there to destroy the church, but to teach. I felt you were there to help priesthood leaders have greater compassion and understanding to a very different problem, a problem we don't have many answers for. You were very articulate and stated your feelings and thoughts very intelligently. I commend you for your integrity and your personal strength.*
>
> *Over the past several years I have given much thought about priesthood leaders in the Church and their lack of understanding for homosexuality. Sadly, I don't believe your story to be uncommon in the Church. I wish that were not true. I hope your comments will be captured in the hearts of those who were sitting around the table that night.*
>
> *Leaders in the Church, like me, are not perfect. I know I have made my share of mistakes. I hope to learn from them. I hope I will always have the love and compassion of Christ as I work with the members of His Church. I know your thoughts will stay with me and will be called upon in the future. I express to you my personal gospel love and an open invitation to church activity. May God be with you and may He continually, as He has done in the past, touch your heart with His love.*
>
> *Sincerely,*
>
> *Terrence Dolin*
> *First Counselor*

The Verdict

Stake Presidency

In the weeks before my court appearance I decided that if I could make a difference with one person it would be worth going through the daunting experience. This man's letter showed me I had made a difference. It gave me hope.

On October 21, I received my formal letter of ex-communication from the Mormon Church. It read:

Dear Sister Freeman:

As you are aware the Portland Oregon East Stake High Council met on September 28, 1999 to consider your case. The judgment of the council was that you be excommunicated from the Church.

Excommunication brings certain restrictions such as: you are not entitled to speak in meetings, offer public prayers, partake of the sacrament, attend any assembly of Church officers, hold an office in the Church, pay tithing and otherwise participate in meetings.

You are encouraged, however, to attend the regular Sunday School, Relief Society, and Sacrament meetings, attend public Conference sessions, live in harmony with gospel standards, and seek for a return to the Church through repentance.

You have the right to appeal this decision. Your appeal should be in writing and sent to me within 30 days.

Excommunication gives you the opportunity to gain complete forgiveness and be worthy to enter the Temple. I urge you to set a daily regimen that includes reading the scriptures and prayer. I invite you to return soon, we need you. I welcome the opportunity to help with your return.

Sincerely,

Mike W. Laboe
Stake President

cc Bishop Weidler

Along with the formal letter of ex-communication, President Laboe sent me a hand written note, which said:

Marnie
I've thoroughly enjoyed getting to know you. You are a delightful young lady with significant value. I am proud of the way you handled yourself. I think your parents would be proud. I hope your interest in the church is soon rekindled. If you need a friend, please call. Mike.

President Mike Laboe treated me with kindness and respect. He is a good man. He is bound by the rules and traditions of the church; however, I feel he did all he could to minimize my discomfort and pain, and I appreciate it to this day.

My life as a Mormon ended that night. I went home and fell into bed.

Chapter 37
You There, God?

I slept hard the night after church court and woke up groggy the next morning. Gradually my new reality set in. I was no longer a Mormon. The church that had enfolded me, kept me safe, and assured me of a home forever with God, had just kicked me out. Even though I had not been active in the church for years, my ex-communication rattled me. My ticket to God's approval had been revoked, my safety net removed. Now what?

As my eyes traced the cracks on the ceiling above my bed, I realized the extent to which I didn't believe God loved me. My head knew He loved all beings, but my heart couldn't feel it was true for me. If it was true, I wanted to know.

It was time to open the conversation and try to find out. Tearfully, I asked, "God, can you love me as a non-Mormon lesbian woman?" I wasn't sure He heard or cared but I had to ask. It was an open-ended question that I hoped would be answered in time.

I got out of bed and sat down in front of my meditation altar. Slipping my Buddhist meditation beads around my neck, I looked at the white porcelain statue of Quan Yin. Peace returned to me as I sat silently and mustered up the strength to face my day.

That night, I fell into another deep sleep. At 1:00 AM I woke with a start, believing someone had just entered my room and taken something important from my bedside table. I sat up and tried to recall what I had left there. I turned on the light and studied my nightstand to find what was missing. Unable to figure it out, I turned off the light and told myself I would look again in the morning.

Two hours later, the same thing happened again.

Night after night, this dream visited me, making me dread going to sleep. Before bed, I would memorize every item on my nightstand, and then would wake up suddenly during the night believing someone had stolen something important from it. It happened over and over and over.

One night, thoughts of my church court kept me awake. In the past, I had often written about what was bothering me. It was therapeutic. So I got out of bed, walked into my study, and turned on my computer. I began to write my story. Before I knew it, it was three in the morning. I felt better and settled back into sleep until the alarm buzzed at seven.

In the back of my mind, though, my struggle about God's love for me continued. I decided to put Him out of my mind - not because I didn't want Him, but because I didn't want to keep feeling bad about Him not wanting me. I would live the best life I possibly could, hoping that one day God would forgive me and want me back.

My life became harder. Grief settled in as a constant companion, and I felt depressed. Even though I had made the right choice to go through my church court, there was a void in my heart that nothing could fill. I couldn't talk to my non-Mormon friends because they couldn't understand the level of loss that overwhelmed me. To them, it seemed illogical to have grief over a church that they felt had treated me unjustly.

To me, I lost much more than just my church; I lost the eternal tie to my family, my friends, my culture, everything that I had been. I was sleep deprived, I was sad, I had a constant feeling of nausea, yet I was determined to survive the path to wherever my heart would lead me.

I continued writing each night. During the day, I would treat patients at my clinic and work with students at the Chinese medicine school. Then I'd go home and force myself to eat dinner. After dinner, I would do guided movements to release my feelings and meditate until I felt enough heaviness lift to write late into the night. Without this daily ritual, I felt too depressed to function.

I made a visit home to my family in Salt Lake City, the first since my ex-communication. The plane landed and I heard the whoosh of air as the plane's door opened. I grabbed my bag from the overhead and was glad for the five-minute walk to where my parents would be waiting for me. I wasn't sure how it would go.

As I walked past security, I saw my mother and father. They had big smiles on their faces. I was surprised by my reaction. I wanted to cry and run to them, to feel their arms wrapped around me like they might have done when I was a girl and had been through rough times. But I wasn't a girl, so I swallowed hard and met their smiles. I hugged them quickly, knowing if I stayed too long the tears would come.

In the way that families do, we avoided the most obvious topic. We never discussed my ex-communication. When Sunday came, I didn't go to the church and, of course, no one protested.

I returned home to the routines I had put in place to keep my body alive, my patients cared for, and my spirit breathing. I continued to write my story at night, and in the morning, I would exercise, meditate and pray to the God I hoped was listening. It got me through each day.

A year passed and my story was written. I felt lighter.

I had heard that part of the therapy of writing can be to burn what you have written as a way to truly be done with the issues you have written about. So one night I took the pages of my story - the story that became this book - to the backyard where I lit a fire in my chiminea, my Mexican terracotta outdoor fireplace. I leaned forward to slip the pages into the flames but couldn't do it. I wasn't willing to have my story end this way. There had to be a happy ending, whatever that would be. I went back upstairs and filed the pages away.

The years flew by. My nightstand dream continued, gradually waning to only two or three nights a week. My clinic was doing well, my work was satisfying, and I had great friends and some romance, too.

Overall, I had reached a place of peace and general happiness.

Chapter 38
Beck

On June 9, 2002, I went on a hike to Falls Creek, a magnificent waterfall on the Washington side of the Columbia River Gorge. My hiking partner was Rebecca Herrin. We hiked, we talked, and we had an incredible time. I felt at peace talking with her, as though I had known her for years. She was hiking in front of me, and I couldn't help but notice her softly muscled, tan legs. She was absolutely gorgeous.

The first time I knew I felt something for Rebecca had been several weeks earlier when we were eating dinner at a restaurant in Hood River. It was a lovely evening, and we'd ordered pan-seared Ahi with wasabi-crusted potatoes. I watched her take a sip of her wine, and when she looked up at me, her eyes sparkled like star-fire emeralds. Uncomfortable with the intensity of my feelings, I broke her gaze, lowered my eyes and tried to re-focus on my food. Driving home that night, I could not get her out of my mind.

After spending the day hiking, we set up camp overlooking the valley. We talked through the evening. The energy between us was electric, and I was beginning to feel something I had not felt in many years.

Once in our sleeping bags, we continued to talk. I found myself telling her about my family, what once was my church, and having been expelled from BYU. She listened quietly, without judgment.

After several more hours of talking, my fingers found hers in the dark. Slowly, I traced the outline of her hand. The lighter my touch, the more I felt. My hand explored hers, and hers mine, as energy pulsed through the deepest fibers of my being.

I fell in love with Rebecca that night.

In September, Rebecca went back to New Hampshire to meet her mother and sister-in-law, Rose, for their annual trip to Smuttynose, on the Isles of Shoals. Although she invited me to go, I decided against it. Based on my own experience with my family, I assumed it would be a long process for Rebecca to tell her family about me, and for them to deal with the fact that I was a woman.

Before she left, I hid notecards in her suitcase for her to open each night. I missed her terribly while she was gone. I was delighted to find similar cards on my nightstand that she had left for me. On the third night at about six, the phone rang. I didn't recognize the number.

"Hello?"

I heard a thick New Hampshire accent say, "Mawnee, this is Becky's motha, Betty. I wanted to call and say hello."

I broke into a big grin. "Hi Betty," I said, "It's nice to meet you."

"It's nice to meet you, Mawnee. Rose and I have just been hearing all about you two. It sounds like you are having a wonderful summa." Then she said, "I wish you could be here with us. We just watched a beautiful sunset."

I couldn't believe it. She wasn't angry, she wasn't judgmental, and she wished I could be there, too. Betty's love for Rebecca was unconditional and she was including me in it. I was being welcomed with open arms like any other member of the family.

Our first year together was magical. We travelled through Italy, shared late night dinners in quirky restaurants in Portland, and made love in the moonlight as we slept outside in the back yard on a cobblestone patio, under a canvas awning.

In December of 2002, Beck and I went home to visit my parents at Christmas. They welcomed us warmly and Beck fit in with my family. We stayed up late each night chatting with my sisters, watching movies with my parents, and sharing Christmas. Late one night my sister Jana said to me, "Rebecca is amazing."

Later that week, we went cross-country skiing to the top of a mountain peak above Park City. We took off our skis and packed down snow for a space to eat lunch. The sky was a pristine blue, and the tall pines swayed gently in the wind as we looked down on Park City. We finished eating and walked over to look at the valley. I took Rebecca in my arms and kissed her. Then I stepped back and looked into her eyes.

"Will you marry me?" I asked.

"Absolutely," she said, holding my gaze.

I had brought two strings of African beads that a woman from Ghana had traded with me for acupuncture treatment. The beads had been made in her village. It was the custom of an engaged woman to wear them until her wedding night.

I tied a string of the small, beautiful beads around Rebecca's waist, and she tied a string around mine. We committed to keeping them on until we were married.

On our drive back to my parent's house, we stopped and had dinner with Grams. She and Rebecca hit if off right away. Grams shared crazy story after crazy story. Just before we left, Grams asked me to tell Rebecca the story about her new skirt. It was a story we had been laughing about for twenty years.

Grams had bought a new polyester suit for church. The skirt was about a foot too long because Grams was just over five feet tall. She was worried the fabric would fray if she cut it. I said, "Grams, I know exactly what we should do."

Actually, I didn't, but I had a solution that made sense to me. I suggested she cut the skirt two inches longer than she wanted the hem to be and let me melt the edges with a match to keep it from fraying. She could then sew her hem. What I didn't realize was how fast polyester burns. I put the first match to the fabric and the flame took off like lightning, scorching my fingers as I rushed to put the blaze out before it crossed the hemline.

Grams asked skeptically, "Marnie, are you sure about this?"

"Yes," I said. "We just need to get some water."

In the end, Gram's hem was barely a quarter of an inch. What we didn't predict was the melted fabric was like a ring of rough plastic that pricked and scratched her legs whenever she wore it, especially when she was sitting in church. She could hardly stand to have it on, but she loved the memory of how it got that way.

As we left, Grams put her arm around Rebecca and said, "Don't ever let Marnie hem any of your clothes."

On July 10, 2003, Rebecca and I committed ourselves to each other with some of our family and friends there to bear witness, including Grams. Even though my parents got lost on the way to the wedding, and we waited an hour-and-a-half for them to arrive, it was the perfect day. I felt complete peace and joy as I looked into Rebecca's eyes and committed to loving her forever.

Chapter 39
Was That A Yes?

As Rebecca and I began planning for our family, I noticed thoughts of God returning. I didn't exactly welcome them because they brought back my feelings that God had betrayed me, but I couldn't put Him out of my mind.

One night as I sat in front of my meditation altar, I felt inspired to write a letter to God to ask a few questions. I asked, "Do you love me, and if you do, why don't I feel it in my heart? And why do I feel heavy and sad, instead of love and light, when I think of You?"

I stopped writing and looked at my statue of Quan Yin, the Goddess of Compassion. She was on my altar but she was not my God. I felt peace and solace when I lit my candle and looked at her face in the shadow. She inspired me to compassion, but to me, God was so much more than that.

I waited there in the candlelight, but no answer came.

Once I was asleep, however, I had an amazing dream. It was so real, I wasn't sure I was dreaming. At about 2:00 AM, I awoke and looked over at my nightstand. In the dream, sitting beside my bed, I saw Jesus. He was sitting on the floor, in a beautiful white robe, with one leg crossed over the other and his arms wrapped around one knee. He was looking to the side, as if he had been waiting a long time, so long that he was not aware I was watching him. He looked different than any of the pictures I had seen of him, though similar. He had an amazing presence of patience, unconditional love and peace. I watched him for a while, and then he faded away.

I woke up and stayed awake the rest of the night. Jesus had been patiently waiting for me to see he was there with me. Maybe there were some things I didn't understand. Maybe things were not as cut and dry as I had been taught. Maybe God was there for me after all.

I rearranged my meditation space to fit the awakening my dream had given me. I kept my porcelain statue of Quan Yin, and added a picture of Christ that belonged to Rebecca's grandmother, as well as a painting of a little boy in Africa holding an empty bowl, waiting for food. I left room for another photo to complete my altar, perhaps an image of Mother Teresa, the Dalai Lama, or even St. Francis of Assisi. I would give myself time to decide.

The dream helped me start to feel God's love in my heart. It was as if God sent me his answer and it was "Yes, Marnie, I do love you as a non-Mormon lesbian woman, and I am here."

Chapter 40
Grams

My grandmother, Lucy Freeman McBride, passed away on August 5th, 2010. She was 95 years old. She spent the last two years of her life in a memory care unit at a retirement center. Prior to that, she did her own gardening, mowing, and housekeeping.

Whenever I went to Salt Lake City, I would visit her. On one visit, I called the nurse to ask if I could take Grams out to lunch.

"She's not been well, Marnie," she said, "but I will ask her."

I waited on the line for several minutes while the nurse talked to Grams. She came back on the line and said, "When I told her Marnie wanted to take her to lunch she said she'd love to go." Then she added, "She may not remember you're coming, though."

My parents warned me that Grams had lost much of her memory and was a shell of who she used to be, at only 90 pounds. I kept all of this in mind as I pulled into the parking lot.

"I'm here to see Lucy McBride," I said to the woman at the counter.

"You must be Marnie," she said. "Your grandmother's been dressed for hours waiting for you. She even had us do her hair. I will go get her."

I heard the sound of little feet shuffling and turned to see Grams coming toward me in high heels. She was wearing a beautiful skirt and jacket and her strawberry blonde hair and make-up were fit for a party. Grams opened her arms and greeted me with the same words I had heard for years, "How are you, sweetie?"

She took my arm and we walked slowly to the car and then went to her favorite restaurant. We ordered lunch but she didn't eat a bite. The outing tired her and I returned her to her room.

I would see her one more time before she passed. On my last visit, she was too weak to get out of bed and her memory was gone. I held her hand as she slept, my beautiful, fragile Grams. Memories swept over me of our times together and all that laughter we'd shared.

Grams took up only about a fourth of the bed, so I crawled in beside her, to lie next to her one last time. As I watched her sleep, she suddenly opened her eyes and looked at me.

"Marnie, I didn't know you were here," she said.

"Yes, Grams. I came to see you," I said.

She looked directly into my eyes and said, "Marnie, I have loved you so much."

I said, "Grams, thank you so much for loving me."

She closed her eyes and drifted off to sleep. I laid by her another couple of hours because I could not bear to leave. I didn't cry. I just lay there loving her with all my heart, amazed that one person could love me so much.

My grandmother's unconditional love created the space for me to eventually love myself. Just one person's belief that I was perfect as I was, with no need to repent or change, opened the doorway for me to believe that I was a worthy human being. I will always be grateful for her life-changing love.

To me, if anyone walked the path of Christ in my life, it was my grandmother. She taught me with her life to love unconditionally, leave judgment to God, choose to be happy, and do in this life whatever it is you want to do.

Grams would be happy I wrote this book. She would be happy with my life because I am happy with it. I enjoy life and people, seek peace and fun, thrive in nature, serve my patients, live honestly, and learn all I can about this beautiful thing we call life. I laugh a lot. I have become able to give kindness and respect to myself, regardless of whether or not I receive it from others.

As I said at the beginning of this book, the pain I endured unraveled me to a degree I couldn't have predicted and certainly wouldn't have wanted. Once unraveled, though, love knit me back together into the woman I was to become and into the devoted partner of Rebecca and the mother of Sophia and Gabriella.

This is a story I must share with anyone who will listen. Thank you for listening.

Epilogue

Rebecca and I moved to the Columbia River Gorge with our two dogs, two cats, and fish. The first night in our new home, we sat on our patio among our trees and flowers gazing at a dark sky filled with stars while listening to two owls *hoo-hoo*, back and forth. I was four months pregnant with our first daughter, Sophia.

We were one day away from leaving for a 3-week trip to India when the news had come that same-sex couples could be married in Portland's Multnomah County. We decided to get legally married before we left for India, just in case the decision was reversed while we were gone.

We called a friend of ours, Mica, an attorney for Multnomah County, and told her we were leaving the following day for India and wanted to get married before we left. While we drove to the courthouse at about 10:30 in the morning on a gray Portland day, she searched for someone to marry us.

As we waited on the County building steps, Rebecca and I laughed about our "shotgun" wedding. I was pregnant, we had planned our marriage that morning, nobody was there but us, and we were on our way out of the country. We were giddy. Finally, we would have all the rights of a legally married couple.

I heard Mica call my name and ask, "Are you ready to get hitched?" Within a few minutes, I looked into Rebecca's eyes for a second time and promised to love her forever, and this time it was *official*.

A month later, when our marriage certificate arrived in the mail, I traced the gold lettering with my finger, feeling incredibly lucky that times had changed. I thought, "We are going to grow old together like any other couple, with the same rights." Our baby would come into a family that would now be legally recognized.

A year later, we received a letter in the mail declaring our marriage null and void. It was an incredibly sad day. This hurt just like those old hurts from the past, and it was easy to go to that place of "things will never really change".

With a little time and perspective, I felt grateful that we held one of the 3,022 same-sex marriage licenses that had been issued. I felt grateful that, even for a short time, we had our indelible rights, like every other human being in the United States.

On Saturday, October 23, 2004 at 6:18 pm, Sophia Rose Freeman came into the world, weighing 6 lbs, 7 oz. Marrying Rebecca was the first greatest day of my life, giving birth to Sophia was the most profound, love-filled day I have ever experienced. I had no idea it was possible to love another being so much.

Then, on January 13, 2009, after moving through an exhausting and heart-wrenching set of adoption hoops, we brought Gabriella home from Guatemala to join our family of two moms, a big sister, two dogs, three cats (a stray moved in) and five chickens. Gabby continues to bring much joy, laughter, and singing to our home.

Our family was complete.

Patiently, we waited ten years, and on May 19, 2014 a U.S. Federal District Court judge ruled that Oregon's 2004 state constitutional amendment banning same-sex marriages violated the Equal Protection Clause of the Federal Constitution. Unfortunately, our marriage was not reinstated, but gay marriage is now legal in the State of Oregon.[2]

---

[2] Mapes, Jeff (May 19, 2014). "Oregon gay marriage ban struck down by

When we heard the news, we took Sophia, who was now age 9, and Gabby, who was 7, to the Portland celebration. I felt it was important for our girls to be a part of history as we celebrated marriage equality.

We listened to Gene Robinson, the first gay Bishop in the Episcopal Church, speak about equal rights. I watched our girls' faces as he talked about equality for all. He congratulated Oregon on passing marriage equality, pointing out that marriage equality passed because of the ten years of work done by both gay and straight people - that it took the cooperation of both.

He then stated, "There is still work to be done, my brothers and sisters; there are still many people who do not have equal rights or protection in the work place. We must all continue to work together until everyone is equal."

As we drove home that night, our girls shared their thoughts about equality. They were surprised that there was inequality in the world. It seemed so "unfair" to them that they could hardly believe it.

I believe the only way we will ever create true equality for all is by educating our children, from the day they are born, that all people are equal and that all people deserve the same inalienable rights.

By definition, legal rights are those bestowed onto a person by a given legal system. Natural rights, on the other hand, are not based upon the laws, customs, or beliefs of any particular culture, government, or religion. They are universal and inalienable.

Below is the definition of "The Family" by the First Presidency of the Mormon church. In many Mormon homes this proclamation is displayed on a large golden plaque. Mormon children are taught that families who do not fit this description are not legitimate families recognized by God, and therefore are not

---

federal judge; same-sex marriages begin". The Oregonian

entitled to the *natural* rights of other families. This seeds inequality. I feel it is important to mention that this belief is not unique to the Mormon church, it is held by most organized religions.

"The Family"

A Proclamation To The World made by The First Presidency And Council of the Twelve Apostles Of The Church Of Jesus Christ Of latter Day Saints.

"We, The First Presidency and the Council of the Twelve Apostles of The Church Of Jesus Christ Of Latter Day Saints, Solemnly proclaim that marriage between a man and a woman is ordained of God and that the family is central to the Creator's plan for the eternal destiny of his children."

"The First Commandment that God gave to Adam and Eve pertained to their potential as husband and wife. We declare that God's commandment for his children to multiply and replenish the earth remains in force. We further declare that God has commanded that the sacred powers of procreation are to be employed only between man and woman, lawfully wedded as husband and wife."

People often ask me about my own birth family. This is something I have chosen to keep sacred. But I will tell you this, there were many difficult years for all of us. There were several years where I thought I had lost them, and I am sure they felt they had lost me. Some of them may argue that I am still lost to them because I am not in the Mormon Church.

As you can imagine, finding out that their eldest daughter and sister was gay was extremely difficult and heartbreaking for them. Understandably, being gay went against their truest heartfelt beliefs and the deepest moral fiber of their being. How could they come to terms with something that was so alien to their core beliefs? I would venture to guess that my being gay is my parent's greatest disappointment.

What I can tell you is about who they have become now. They love me deeply. They love Rebecca, and they love our girls just as they love the other grandchildren in our family. We are welcomed in the same way the rest of my family is welcomed. My family is there for us unconditionally, offering to help and support us in every way possible.

As difficult as it was to have a gay daughter, and a gay sister, they have chosen to love me anyway.

Yes, it is true that they hope one day I will change and go back to the church. I believe this will always be their hope. I have learned to accept this about them, and they have learned to accept me.

I love my family with all of my heart, each one of them. When it comes to my brothers and sisters, I feel the same love and protection for them that I have for my own children; I would give them all that I have and I love them unconditionally, which I believe is the foundation of religion - to love all people as Christ has loved.

It is too bad that from the time we are little children religion teaches us that homosexuality is an abomination before God. We are taught to believe in a harsh God that has no place for people like us in His Kingdom. We are taught that being gay, lesbian or transgender is equal to the gravest of sins like murder and pedophilia. We are told that people like us lead to the undoing of the moral fiber of this country, the institution of family and marriage, and life as we know it. If these are the teachings of our churches, it is no wonder that people respond with judgments and unkindness.

Because of what we have been taught, we begin to believe that who we are is inherently evil, and we feel unworthy as human beings. We believe we are not a part of God's plan, and that we must be some kind of terrible mistake, that somehow we must repent and change ourselves or we will be forever damned. We begin to believe we are unworthy of our rights as human beings, unworthy of God's love, and even unworthy of life itself.

Recently, in an interview with a newspaper reporter, I was

asked if times had changed, or could some of the things that have happened in the past still happen.

As my answer, I shared a story about my oldest daughter Sophia, when the mother of her first friend in kindergarten found out she had two Moms:

Sophia started kindergarten in September of 2010. She chose one of her many pink outfits to wear on her first day. We woke at 6:30 AM sharp. She jumped out of bed, put on her new clothes, ate her breakfast as quickly as she could, and was ready to go forty-five minutes early, which meant forty-five minutes of hearing "How much longer?" As we drove to school, she was a buzz of excitement.

Beck and I both drove her to school that first day. We were excited, too. Opening her car door, she jumped out in her new dress with a new backpack and matching lunch bag. She slipped her little hand in mine as we walked into her school. I glanced down at her and noticed her eyes were getting larger with every step we took.

When I opened the front door, her little face went pale. Her excitement had turned to fear. She was glued to my leg as her new teacher came to say hello.

Sophia begged me to take her home. I smiled that mom kind of smile, kissed her on the head, and promised I would pick her up after school. I pried her hands off and walked away without looking back. Leaving her that first time felt like I had left a piece of my heart. I admit, Rebecca and I had tears in our eyes.

I was twenty minutes early to pick her up and waited nervously outside. When the teacher led the class out, I walked over to Sophia. I looked in her little blue eyes and saw the sadness of a six-year old whose idea of school didn't measure up. I put my arm around her as we walked to the car.

"How'd your first day go?" I asked.

She held her answer until we were inside the car, then burst into tears. "I don't have any friends. There's no one to sit by in class, no one to play with at recess, and no one to sit by at lunch."

It was all I could do not to burst into tears myself.

The weeks wore on as we continued to take her to school in the morning, kiss her goodbye, and walk away without looking back. Each day, she seemed sadder. Sophia is a gentle little soul. She's the kid that lets others go first. It is easy for her to disappear.

Weeks turned into months, and still no friends. Home schooling began to look like a great option. I could hardly stand her pain.

In a flash it all changed. One day I picked Sophia up as usual. Instead of a sad little face, she came skipping toward me with a huge grin. She was singing, "I have a new friend, I have a new friend, I have a new friend!"

Sophia and Jessica, an equally shy little girl, had found each other. From that day forward school became something Soph looked forward to and loved.

Each morning when I dropped Sophia off at school, Jessica would hide behind the classroom door and jump out to give her a big hug. Their friendship blossomed over the next few months and kindergarten became a great experience. It's amazing how one friend can make all the difference.

In the Columbia River Gorge, from November to February, the weather is extreme. Wind whips at 60 mph and the rain blows sideways. Sophia and Jessica would come out of school carrying their coats with Sophia's lunch box and backpack stacked over the handle of Jessica's wheeled backpack. I would quickly put their coats on, give them hugs, and separate all of their belongings as they hugged each other goodbye. This became our after-school ritual.

Eventually, Jessica's older sister joined us in this ritual. I could see they were both sweet little girls. One day Jessica's older sister asked, "Is it true that Sophia has two moms?"

"Yes," I said. "Her other mom is Rebecca."

Coincidentally, Sophia and Jessica had swapped phone numbers that day because they wanted to have a play date. Rebecca called and left a message for Jessica's mom asking to get the girls together.

The following day we received a handwritten note from Jessica's mother inviting Sophia to a class that was taught each week in their Southern Baptist church. We called and left a message explaining that their church meeting was too late on a school night during the middle of a week for Sophia to attend. We asked if we could schedule a play date instead, maybe at the park or the gymnastics gym, or maybe their family would come to our house for dinner.

We didn't receive a response to our call.

A couple of days later when I dropped Sophia off at school, Jessica did not jump out from behind the door. Instead, she looked at me and said, "Does Sophia really have two moms?"

Soph said, "Yes, I have Mumma B (B for Beck) and I have my Mom."

I said, "Yes, isn't she lucky she has two moms instead of just one?"

Jessica looked distraught for a moment and then said, "Oh." She took Sophia's hand and off they went.

I began to notice a difference in our after-school ritual. Jessica and her sister would be their friendly selves until their mother arrived. Then they would step back from us and look away as their mother whisked them off.

Sophia continued begging for play dates, so we tried again. Eventually Rebecca reached Jessica's dad and he said "We aren't letting Jessica have any play dates right now." By now we had a pretty good idea there was a problem with having two moms.

I hoped if Jessica's mom continued to see us every day, if she saw that we were friendly and very normal like everyone else, we could win her over.

About a week later, as I was pulling Sophia's lunch bag off Jessica's rolling backpack, I was pushed from behind. Jessica's mother was in absolute rage as she reached around and grabbed Sophia's lunch bag and shoved it at me. She grabbed Jessica by her upper arm and led her to the car.

I looked down at Sophia and saw a look that is hard to describe. It was a mixture of hurt, fear, and shock.

I dropped Sophia off at school the following morning and Jessica wasn't there. I kissed her goodbye and saw Jessica's mom in the school office as I walked to my car. I smiled and politely said hello.

She said, "I've taken Jessica and her sister out of this horrible school."

Sophia and Jessica didn't get to say goodbye and we never saw Jessica again.

Sophia was heartbroken when the teacher told her Jessica was not going to be in class anymore. She sobbed as we drove home after school.

School became lonely for Sophia again. She cried herself to sleep each night and begged each day to call Jessica. One day I said we could call. Jessica answered the phone and the two little girls were thrilled to be together again, talking like nothing had ever changed.

"Who are you talking to," asked Jessica's mother in the background.

"Sophia," said Jessica.

"Hang up right now," said her mother.

Jessica said, "Bye," and the line went dead.

Over the next few months, Sophia called Jessica several more times. Jessica's mother would answer the phone, tell Sophia that Jessica couldn't talk to her, and then hang up.

Sophia asked me why Jessica's mom wasn't kind. I explained that she would not let Sophia and Jessica be friends because she was missing some kindness in her heart, that she didn't understand how important their friendship was to them.

Soph said, "If her Mom would just give me a chance, she would see what a good friend I could be. Mom, please would you call her and ask her to just give me a chance?"

She begged me to call Jessica's mother. I said "I can't, Soph. There is nothing I can do to change her mind."

I don't know if I handled this the right way. Should I have told my six-year old that because she has two moms some people are not going to like her? In fact, some people will dislike her moms so much that they will not let their kids play with her? I didn't tell her the truth of why Jessica was gone, even though I believe the truth is the way to go, even when it is painful. I was not willing to put any thought into her mind that she was not okay because she has two moms. At this point, she freely states that she has two moms, with no worry of any type of consequence. The reality will come soon enough.

A year passed and she was no longer crying herself to sleep, but when she is quiet just before sleep, she still thinks of Jessica and how much she misses her. "Mom," she said, "I feel like I am okay during the day, most of the time, but at night sometimes Jessica comes to me in my dreams, and then I miss her so much."

I do believe we are beginning to see cracks in this issue in fundamentalist religions. States are passing Same-Sex Marriage bills, and the LGBT community is standing together as never before.

I can only hope people will look within their own hearts, consider how they themselves would like to be treated, and leave judgment to someone much greater than themselves. If people will open their hearts, they will see we are all the same. We have the same heartaches, dreams and desires, like any other human being.

I have found a different God, an *unconditionally* loving God where each of us is worthy, loved and accepted. I believe that as human beings, God's love is our birthright. My hope is that my story may help others as they face their fears and become their greatest selves, even if that ends up being only one person - to the one.

Recently I had a conversation with my sister and her husband. The topic of choice came up, the choice to be homosexual. They believe I made the choice to be lesbian, and that if I would simply change my choice, everything would be all right again.

I looked at my brother-in-law and quietly asked, "When did you make your choice?"

"What?" he said, panicked that I thought he had made a choice not to be gay.

I let the words hang in the air. Then he said, "Oh, I get it." In that moment he realized I didn't make a choice either.

I wish everyone could understand that we don't choose who we are.

I didn't choose to be lesbian. I was born lesbian. It is my normal.

Grams once said to me, "Marnie, you can do in this life whatever it is you want to do, I know it." She was right, and I have.

The same is true for you.

This is What I Know

1. Happiness is a choice; we make that choice every day. (Lucy Freeman McBride)
2. Love people unconditionally. (Lucy Freeman McBride)
3. Whatever you set your mind to, you can accomplish. (Lucy Freeman McBride)
4. Being gay or lesbian is not something we choose; it is who we are.
5. I need to have spirituality in my life in order to feel whole.
6. We must forgive. It is the only way we will find happiness.
7. Leave what we don't understand to God, let him be the judge. (Lucy Freeman McBride)
8. How we treat others, including humans, animals, and even our planet, is the truest representation of following Christ.
9. There is not one right way.
10. There is not one path to God.
11. When you need to say you're sorry, just do it.
12. Create a space for prayer and meditation.
13. In order to heal, we must feel what we feel.
14. Write what you feel, it helps get it out of you.
15. Sit with yourself, and you can heal your heart.
16. God loves every one of us, even me, even you.
17. If what you are doing is not the path of your heart, it is not your path.

18. You can do whatever you set your mind to.
19. As a human, you deserve the same indelible rights as every other human.
20. Don't compromise on your deal breakers just for love. Vet potential partners against it. Mine are family, spirituality, following the path of my heart, loving animals, and loving the outdoors.

Made in the USA
Middletown, DE
27 June 2018